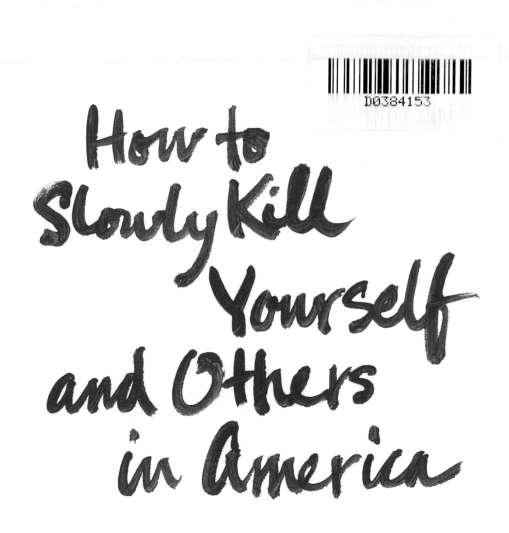

How to
Slowly Kill
Yourself
and Others
in America

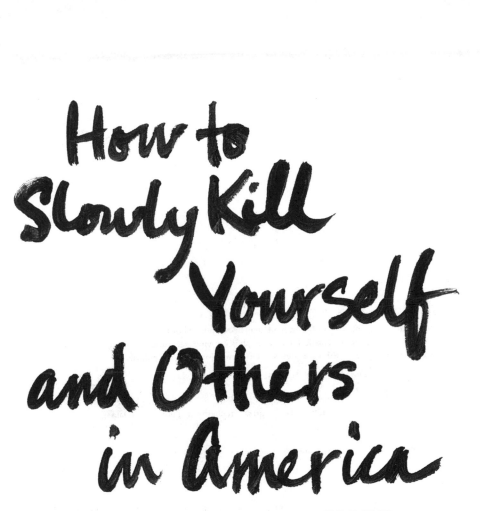

How to Slowly Kill Yourself and Others in America

ESSAYS

Kiese Laymon

BOLDEN

AN AGATE IMPRINT

CHICAGO

Library of Congress Cataloging-in-Publication Data

Laymon, Kiese.

How to slowly kill yourself and others in America / by Kiese Laymon.

pages cm

Includes index.

Summary: "A collection of essays on family, race, violence, celebrity, music, writing, and other topics"-- Provided by publisher.

ISBN 978-1-932841-77-0 (pbk.) -- ISBN 1-932841-77-6 (pbk.) -- ISBN 978-1-57284-726-2 (ebook) --   ISBN 1-57284-726-3 (ebook)

1. Laymon, Kiese. 2. African American novelists--Biography. 3. African American teachers--Biography. 4. Jackson (Miss.)--Biography. I. Title.

PS3612.A959Z46 2013

813'.6--dc23

[B]

                    2013019503

9 8 7 6

Bolden Books is an imprint of Agate Publishing. Agate books are available in bulk at discount prices. For more information, visit agatepublishing.com.

For my family, my students, and Mississippi.

Table of Contents

*"Morally, there has been no change at all,
and a moral change is the only real one."*

—James Baldwin

Author's Note

I STARTED WRITING THIS BOOK NEARLY SIX YEARS AGO. My first novel, then titled *My Name Is City*, had been picked up by a major New York publisher, but I was slowly coming to understand that the novel I wanted to be read would never be published. I put everything I ever imagined into that novel, because I couldn't see myself living beyond thirty-two years old.

While the editorial process slowed, picked back up, and eventually stopped, I was getting worse at being human. One cold night in New York, someone I loved told me that I was precisely the kind of human being I claimed to despise. I defended myself against this truth, and really against responsibility, as American monsters and American murderers tend to do, and I tried to make this person feel as absolutely worthless, confused, and malignant as I was. Later that night, I couldn't sleep, and for the first time in my life, I wrote the sentence, "I've been slowly killing myself and others close to me."

A year or two after I started this book, I realized I wanted my work to be a site of the catastrophic and pleasurable, the intellectual and the everyday, the public and the private, the awkwardly destructive and the wholly sublime. Instead of imagining standard "literary" audiences, I knew that I wanted to question the traditional literary fictive trajectory by writing to folks (or sensibilities) who don't read for a living *and* those folks (or sensibilities) who are paid to read for a living, in everything I created. I knew that I wanted to create work that explored, with colorful profundity and comedy, the reckless order of American human being, especially since so much of the nation was in a dizzying rush to crown itself multicultural, post-racial, and mostly innocent.

I didn't know much of what I wanted in the way of shape from the book, but I knew I didn't want my voices to be the only voices in the book. I couldn't find literary models of what I wanted to do, but I had plenty of musical models. Like a lot of black men who made it through the 80s and 90s, I always wanted to be an emcee. For me, this was partially because most American literature, unlike lots of American blues, soul, and hip-hop, did not create an echo. Most American literary classics were not courageous, imaginative, or honest enough to imagine our people or our experiences as parts of its audience. These classics were lauded, canonized, but I rarely found them genius, responsible, or even interesting. Conversely, black American musical genius necessitated that we work with it, so much so that our experiences and imaginations almost became indistinguishable from the actual musical work itself.

But when I did find brilliant, soulful, courageous, black American literature, it imagined us as its readers, and those literary echoes saved my life. As much as hip-hop and the blues inspired me, my most meaningful discoveries about the act of being human have come through the solitary act of listening to turning pages, rereading clumsy passages, and marking up the sides of shifty text. It wasn't the text alone that did the work; it was the reading, and rereading, of the text that necessitated the work. Rereading *The Bluest Eye* taught me how to see. Rereading *The Fire Next Time* taught me how to love. Rereading *Going to the Territory* taught me that "human being" was a verb. Rereading *Kindred* taught me to will myself beyond spectacle and into generative imagination that needed to look forward and back.

While hundreds of my favorite songs and albums reminded me that I was not alone, that American genius was real, that American sound could be this magical communal site of resistance and activism, listening to black American music seldom made me want to be better at being human. This has everything to do with what I chose to listen to, and very little to do with the totality of our music. I know, for example, that the music of Mahalia Jackson kept my grandma, mother, and aunts alive and committed to love. I know that without black American music, particularly the music of the black church in the Deep South, we would have been killed and/or continued killing ourselves a lot faster.

Still, I wanted to produce a book with a Mississippi blues and gospel ethos. And I wanted to shape the book in the form of some of my favorite albums. I thought of the essays as tracks. I thought of some of the pieces in the book as songs with multiple voices and layered musicality. I thought of ways to bring the ad lib, riff, collaboration, and necessary digression to the page. I wanted a book that could be read front to back in one setting. I wanted to explore the benefits and burdens of being born a black boy in America without the predictable literary rigidity. And I wanted young black Southerners, particularly, to generate art in response to this text while working with the essays at being better at being human. The hardest part, of course, is that I wanted to be honest about my family, my nation, my region, my memory, and me.

I'm not sure I've done anything I hoped to do, but I'm thankful you've given the voices and sentences in my blood, a chance to work with you. This is how to slowly kill yourself and others in America.

Kiese Laymon
May 17, 2013

Prologue

We Will Never Ever Know: Letters to Uncle Jimmy

DEAR UNCLE JIMMY,

As a black boy growing up in Mississippi, I learned that there was a rickety bridge between right and wrong. And I learned that I would be disciplined more harshly than white boys for even slightly leaning toward the wrong side. But like you, Uncle Jimmy, I sadly didn't give a fuck. I broke bets I made with myself, got kicked out of high school a number of times, was suspended from college, and had run-ins with police that broke Mama and Grandma's heart. Unlike you, though, I did all of this in close proximity to a lanky, living, breathing warning.

Uncle Jimmy, that warning was you.

On July 4, you threw down your crack pipe, scrubbed yourself clean, and bought my grandma some meat. "This Mama's meat," you wrote in loopy black letters on a bloody paper sack. When your sister, my mama, called me in my office at Vassar in Poughkeepsie, New York, she had no idea that the Fourth of July would be the last day she would see you alive.

You joked with your sisters before taking little Tre to get more bottle rockets. Reeking of that familiar mix of sour scalp and Jordan cologne, you probably blinked those huge webbed eyes more than usual and actually asked questions of our family.

As with many of Mama's stories, you weren't the star, but you were the precocious, literally paroled man on whom our family's emotional stability truly rested. There was a terrible clarity in Mama's voice when she told me the story of July 4. Mama's voice sounded like this any time you followed a crack binge or a run-in with the police with something graceful like leading a Sunday school session or using your pension to buy that house over off Highway 35.

"You driving my sister crazy now," Aunt Sue told me, more than twenty years ago, the night I drove my mama into a nervous breakdown. "You heading down that same road as Jimmy."

I learned that night that the Uncle Jimmy road ran adjacent to the refined, curbed avenues that nearly all sisters, aunts, mamas, and grandmas want their black boys to travel. Aunt Sue and Mama wanted me to know, without a doubt, that whatever consumed you would eventually consume me unless I prayed diligently, obeyed the law, remained clean, and got out of Mississippi by any means necessary. But even as I sprinted away from Mississippi to Ohio, then Indiana, and now New York, if I looked down I could never really distinguish your footprints from my own.

That's what I felt before July 7.

On July 7, three days after you toted that bag of meat to Grandma's house, I got a call. Grandma was looking for you. She drove over to your house because you wouldn't answer the phone. Grandma opened the screen and pounded on your door that evening. She yelled your name over and over again, but you didn't answer.

You couldn't.

On July 12, eight days after you brought Grandma her bloody meat, your sisters walked into Mapp Funeral Home and readied your body, the body of Grandma's first child, and their only brother, for public viewing. My mama made the funeral director change your shirt.

Your sister, Sue, the most mesmerizing preacher in Mississippi, eulogized you in Concord Baptist Church. We were all baptized there. At the core of Sue's eulogy were three ideas: 1) "Niggers" do not exist. 2) Perfectly sanitized, wholly responsible black people do not exist. 3) You, Jimmy Alexander, were equally wicked and wonderful and had far more in common with us than we wanted to admit.

Aunt Sue made the church know that you lived a life of bad; not bad meaning good, or bad meaning evil, but bad meaning bad at being human. In traditional Old Testament style, she explored justice and recreated in you someone who had prepared himself for death by finally accepting and earning life in the days before your passing. Sue told the church the story of your bringing that meat to Grandma's house. She told us that you had gotten your finances in order.

"Jimmy wasn't that different from anyone in this church," she told us. "No better or no worse. And that's what we have to accept. He was racing toward death, but he was a part of our family. He was all of our brother."

While Sue stood in the pulpit teaching us about acceptance of our badness, I realized that you were the only child of Grandma's who did not become a teacher. If you had taught for a living, you might not have been any physically or emotionally healthier, since we know that occupations are never shields from reckless sex, drug abuse, cowardice, deceptiveness, and desperation. But Grandma would have found far more peace on the day of your funeral if she knew her oldest child, a big-eyed black boy born in the late 1940s, taught somebody somewhere something before he died.

As Grandma's youngest daughter gave the church words to lean on, your mother, our teacher, the thickest, most present human being either of us has known, folded up at the end of the pew. Grandma cried herself breathless as your bloodless body lay right over the site of your baptism. I held Grandma, though, Uncle Jimmy. I held her just like she would have wanted you to hold her if I were stretched out in that casket.

I needed you, Uncle Jimmy. I needed you the day of your funeral. And when we were both alive, I needed you to be better than you were, but I never loved you enough to tell you. I could have shown you by calling you more, or walking with you down Old Morton Road when I visited during the summer and at Christmas. We could have wondered about the widened roads and the huge dying trees we both imagined fighting off Godzilla and Starscream. We could have joked and tossed ironic jabs back and forth as some nephews and uncles do.

Then, if we really cared, we could have harnessed the courage to knock each other's hustles.

I could have finally said, "Uncle Jimmy, you drowning yourself with that crack and all that hate. Ain't nothing really behind your smile, man. I love you and I need you to live." And you could have told me, "There's more than one way to drown, nephew. You looking pretty wet yourself. I know I'm under that water. You know where you at?"

But those words were never said. We talked, but we didn't reckon with each other. Hence, all of our communication created no meaningful reverberation outside our speculations about each other. The last thing you said to me the Christmas before you died was, "No matter how much right you try to do, white folks do everything they can to make a nigga remember they owned us." There was a silence after that sentence, and I filled that silence with a mechanical nod of my head and a weak, "Yeah. I hear that."

By that point, though, I believed I knew you. I assumed that you coped with the weight of a paroled life as a black man in Mississippi by laughing, acting a fool, relying on crack cocaine, alcohol, and the manipulation of women who were just as hopeless as you. And I assumed that you knew that I'd started coping in many of the same ways. One of the only differences between you and me was that I fell deeply in love with the possibilities of written and spoken words. I used words to create stories, essays, and novels I thought you'd want to read, hear, and see.

When I wasn't writing things that you might have wanted or needed to read, hear, and see, I created fictive versions of you that were, sadly, more interesting and more loving than I ever allowed you to be in real life. You inspired thousands of paragraphs, hundreds of scenes, but I never showed you one single sentence. I was afraid to know for sure that you thought my work was my hustle—a shinny, indulgent waste of time. But more than that, I didn't want you to know that I wanted you to be better at being human.

I didn't want you to see that I saw in the real you someone I never wanted to be, a shiftless paroled "nigger" worthy of only hollow awe or rabid disgust, a smiling "nigger" who fought a few good rounds before getting his ass whupped by white supremacy and quaint multiculturalism over and over again. Uncle Jimmy, I knew that you were slowly killing yourself. And predictably, I knew that I would become you.

I hated you and me both for that.

This is a shameful admission, a confession that is even more sour with indulgent guilt when I acknowledge that all of the women in my writing who are partially based on the characters of Grandma, Mama, Aunt Sue, and Aunt Linda are far less moving, round, and paradoxical than the actual women themselves. And this has less to do with my writing than it does with my love and understanding of these human beings, and our love and understanding of each other. I loved the women in our family enough to ask them questions. They loved me enough to answer those questions, often with questions of their own. I wrote to them. They wrote back.

Echo.

Honestly, I don't know if I ever asked you any real questions other than why you looked so happy in your Vietnam pictures, when I was ten, and why you said, "There's some fine bitches on earth," when you picked me up from grad school when I was twenty-four.

My creating interesting American characters based on you to fit the specifications of a paragraph doesn't make me despicable; it makes me an American writer. What makes me despicable is that one of the responsibilities of American writers is to broaden the confines, sensibilities, and generative capacity of American literature by broadening the audience to whom we write, and hoping that broadened audience writes back with brutal imagination, magic, and brilliance.

Echo.

You can't really explore the terror and wonder of being born, as Baldwin says, "captive in the supposed Promised Land" if one never conceives of the captives as the crucial critics, not simply consumers or objects, of one's work. I started writing this book to you before you died. I was in desperate need of echo and I'd convinced myself that the only way to live was to write through what was helping me kill myself. I don't only wish you could have read this book, Uncle Jimmy; I wish you could have written back to us.

Anyway, only a fool doesn't actively regret. I wish we could have waded in the awkward acceptance that we are neither African nor conventionally American; neither subhuman nor superhuman; neither tragic nor comic; neither defeated nor victorious. I wish we could have affirmed our awareness that our blackness and our Southerness are both perpetual burden and benefit, and our masculinity and femininity something that must be perpetually reckoned with.

Mostly, Uncle Jimmy, I wish you could have told me that we are fucked up, and much of the nation has always wanted it that way, but we owe it to our teachers and our children to imagine new routes into beauty, health, compassion, citizenry, and American imagination. We owe it to each other to love and insist on meaningful revision until the day we die.

That's what I needed to tell you when you were alive. That's what I needed you to show me. That's what I need help believing.

One night, while revising *Long Division,* I thanked God that you weren't my father, while feeling like the luckiest nephew in the world because I could call someone as tortured as you my uncle. I wondered who and what I really would have become without you as my warning. I wondered how your life would have been different if I had told you I loved you. What would you have done differently with your life if you had really believed me? What would we have both felt? If you wrote truthfully to me, how would you start and end your letter? What senses would you write through? What would you discover?

Uncle Jimmy, no matter how I contort these words and squeeze the mess out of my memory and imagination, we will never ever know. This book is a love letter written a few years too late. I am sorry I didn't love you.

Your nephew,
Kiese

***

Dear Jimmy,

Although you have transitioned to the other side of life, I still feel your presence and pray for you. Our nephew, Kiese, thinks he lives with your ghost. I try to tell him that he's always lived with your spirit.

I have learned more about you in death than I knew in life. Little did I know that a young lady you used to smoke crack with has come to know Jesus and become a part of my ministry. We never know what our lives will bring to those we leave behind.

I never questioned your love for me or for the family. I knew you loved us, but I was never sure if you loved yourself. Life has a way of rewinding itself.

You once said to me from your hospital bed that it wasn't so much the crack as the sex that kept you getting high. My life had not trained my mind to understand or accept your logic. I left the hospital after midnight out of frustration and disappointment at how you did not value your life. I said to you, "If you don't care about you, why should I?" I walked out of the hospital wondering what I could do to help my brother. God gave me the answer. "Love him," He said. "Demand greatness of him and give him to me." I learned another lesson from you that night. Love requires forgiveness, truth, high expectations, and patience.

You taught me something very important that night. You taught me that love without acceptance and understanding isn't love. I told you the next morning that I would not give you money under any circumstance. If you were hungry, I would feed you. If you were lonely, I would share scriptures and words of encouragement. But I would not cast my pearls to the swine. I would not give you my hard-earned cash to purchase drugs.

You fought your demons, Jimmy, and I've fought mine. This young lady called me crying a little past midnight. She wanted me to know about you. She told me that while you were getting high you encouraged her to reclaim her life and her children. She said, "Mr. Jimmy was a good man. He tried to help people. Often people took his kindness as a weakness." She told me of how you gave her money to buy her children clothes and how you counseled her about the importance of raising her children and setting a good example for them.

I want you to know she took your advice. She is now off crack and her children are living with her. Life is a struggle at times but she is determined to make it. You made a difference in her life. You made a difference in mine.

I was so glad that the last time that we spoke, you told me you didn't hate white people anymore. For the first time in my life, you seemed to be at peace. Peace with yourself, Mama, the family, and peace with your God.

You didn't look like the man who had grown old too soon, with the stressors of life written in every wrinkle in your face. You did not look like a man with less than 90 percent lung and heart capacity. Somehow, some way, your youth had returned. Your dignity was restored and you had become the man you wanted to be all your life. You looked like the handsome brother of your youth. Mary commented as we waved goodbye on that Fourth of July, "Do you think Jimmy is about to die?" I did not respond but I knew that life as you knew it had come to its final hours.

One day when I was leaving the VA Hospital, you told me you wanted me to preach at your funeral. I told you that you were crazy and that was one thing that I would never do. Well, you never ever know what love and God makes possible.

On July 12, I stood looking into a casket that belonged to my brother. I stepped from the clothes of being your sister and put on the robes of an ambassador for God. I shared the hope of a man who struggled, won, and lost, who was often too lonely to face life while married to a pipe filled with crack. While cleaning out your home, I found your journal. I read your words and I felt your pain in ways *that I will never be able to express. What you could not articulate in life you spoke to us from your journals. You wrote, "I have stolen from my mother, hurt my sisters and I want to stop but I don't know how." On another page you wrote, "I don't know the person I have become. God help me."*

Your heart was good but you forgot to guard it. You killed yourself slowly because of this. The heart is the true measure of a man or woman. I loved you and I know that you knew I loved you. We all have addictions. Some are just more obvious to the eye. We are all dying, but we are all living. The key is to live with as much dignity as you can and never ever bring other people down because you've given up on life. Your work is finished but your worth is still being revealed. Your life was not in vain, Jimmy. You made a difference. You helped our mother find the strength and the courage to fight another day and your words inspired her to change her life. I think that is the true measure of our worth and why God put us on the earth. Have we made life better for others by lending a hand, a heart, a word, a song, hope for despair— and always, always shared the gift of love? We may be broken, but God knows how to mend broken hearts and spirits. I have been made better by knowing you, brother, and I thank you for the lessons along the way.

Love always,

Your sister Sue

The Worst of White Folks

AY BACK IN THE DAY, WHEN TWITTER WAS A bootleg reindeer name, David Rozier invented farting during Mass. A few minutes *before* we marveled at the six Catholics at Holy Family Catholic School sipping out of one gold goblet, and right *after* Father Joe suggested we offer each other "a sign of peace," David tapped me on my shoulder, swung his right arm around his back and farted in his hand. Father Joe rolled his eyes from the pulpit as David proceeded to shake the hands of Ms. Bockman, Ms. Raphael, and all the other sixth- and seventh-graders in our row.

Side by side, David and I looked as different as two Mississippi black boys could look. He reminded me of a shorter version of my cousin Jermaine, who lived up in Chicago. David had the forearms and calves of a wiry point guard, with the teeniest head you'd ever seen in your life. He had bright, curious, clear eyes, a voice that was octaves deeper than you'd expect, and these elephant ears that Angela Williams would pluck on field trips. David wasn't the flyest dresser in the seventh grade, but he—like our boy Lerthon—came to school fabric-softener fresh with just a whiff of fried eggs and canned biscuits. I, on the other hand, was slightly less husky than the Human Beat Box and smelled like stale sweat and off-brand dishwashing soap.

The day David offered us his sign of peace, Ms. Bockman, who initially thought David was finally being respectful of Catholic tradition, went off on me in homeroom. When I wouldn't tell her why I was laughing, she walked me into the hallway and pointed down to the principal's office.

"Kiese, you're not giving me a choice," she said. "Move it!"

As I walked down the hall to the principal's office with Ms. Bockman at my side, our homeroom door opened behind us.

"Hold up!" It was David Rozier. "Kiese ain't do nothing," he told Ms. Bockman. "It's my bad he was laughing. I'm responsible."

I looked at David and waited for something more, something familiar.

I got nothing

David just stood there swaying with his peanut head tucked into his chest. He wouldn't stop tracing the brown splotches on the floor with his toe.

Since fourth grade, David Rozier and I had spent every day calling and responding, daring each other to revise all the rules of Mississippi juvenile delinquency. We were the Run-DMC of bad behavior at Holy Family Catholic School, and Lerthon was our Jam Master Jay. But in that second, I was a spectator, a confused fan. Hard as I tried, I couldn't understand the movement, language, and work of American responsibility, especially coming from the mouth of David Rozier.

"I made Kiese laugh in Mass," David told Ms. Bockman.

"But you didn't laugh," she said.

"I passed gas in my hand and I spread it," I remember David saying without a smirk. I busted out laughing again. "Kiese wouldn't be laughing without me. I'm saying I'm responsible."

While we sat outside the principal's office waiting for the secretary to call our mamas, I joked that I saw Ms. Bockman smell her hand. David wouldn't laugh. After a minute or two of forced yawning to break the silence, I asked David why he'd accepted responsibility for my acting a fool.

"I don't even know," I remember him saying. "Coach Stanley said we gotta be more responsible for our team, and my grandma said I gotta start acting responsible, too. I forgot at first. Then I remembered."

I couldn't understand.

David and I got suspended from our rickety black Catholic school that day. Later that evening, in our black neighborhoods, our mothers called their mothers. Under our grandmothers' guidance, our backs, elbows, knees, necks, and thighs were destroyed. We now knew that the worst whupping you could get was the playing-fart-games-in-Catholic-church whupping. We figured it was our mothers' way of keeping us out of black gangs, black prisons, black clinics, black cemeteries. We knew it was their way of proving to our grandmothers that they were responsible.

The licks, during my whupping at least, were in sync with every syllable out of Mama's mouth.

At least twenty-five solid syllables. At least twenty-five stinging licks.

Near the second half of the whupping, Mama, who was usually reckless with her belt, channeled the precision of Grandma and dropped ten licks to the words, "don't…you…know…white… folks…don't…care…if…you…die…"

Even as a juvenile delinquent who didn't fully understand what "responsibility" meant, I understood that when Mama said "white folks," she meant *the worst of white folks*. I knew this literally because there were so many different types of white folks on television, and the only white folks I knew personally at the time—Ms. Bockman, Ms. Jacoby, Ms. Raphael, and Lori Bakutis—were complicated, caring white folks who didn't want me dead. The truth was that you didn't have to know white folks personally to understand what *the worst of white folks* nudged your family to feel and do.

The worst of white folks, I understood, wasn't some gang of rabid white people in crisp pillowcases and shaved heads. *The worst of white folks* was a pathetic, powerful "it." It conveniently forgot that it came to this country on a boat, then reacted violently when anything or anyone suggested it share. *The worst of white folks* wanted our mamas and grandmas to work themselves sick for a tiny sliver of an American pie it needed to believe it had made from scratch. It was all at once crazy-making and quick to discipline us for acting crazy. It had an insatiable appetite for virtuoso black performance and routine black suffering. *The worst of white folks* really believed that the height of black and brown aspiration should be emulation of itself. White Americans were wholly responsible for *the worst of white folks*, though they would make sure it never wholly defined them.

I didn't know a lot as a seventh-grader in Mississippi, and I had far fewer words to describe what I actually knew, but *the worst of white folks* I knew far too well. David Rozier and I both did.

It passed through blood.

***

Up in Maywood, Illinois, which is about ten miles west of downtown Chicago, my first cousin, Jermaine, was just as familiar with *the worst of white folks* as we were in Jackson. Though the winters were colder, the vowel sounds shorter, the buildings taller, and the yards a lot smaller, the Chicago I visited as a child always felt like an orange piece of Mississippi that had broken off and floated away…with one major exception.

Whereas the mid-twentieth century saw millions of black Americans leave Alabama, Louisiana, and Mississippi for Chicago, Indianapolis, Milwaukee, Gary, and Detroit, by the mid-1980s we were in the midst of a much less concentrated reverse migration. Chicago's Vice Lords and Folks had made their way into Jackson and Memphis.

When David and I started the seventh grade, we heard rumors that rocking your hat tilted to the left or right, doing twisted things with your fingers, and wearing the wrong colors were grounds for a beatdown. But by the end of seventh grade, the rumors became full-fledged law in Jackson. As much as this law immediately altered the way David, Lerthon, Henry Wallace, and I moved through space near the end of seventh grade, this law sadly governed Jermaine's entire life in Chicago.

My father took me to visit my aunt, Jermaine, and his siblings the summer I turned fourteen. We didn't stay long, but the whole time I was there, I kept hoping that Jermaine would come back to stay with me in Jackson. I figured that girls like Marsha Middleton, who wouldn't give me much rhythm, would have to pay attention if they knew I was cool enough to have a cousin like Jermaine.

Jermaine carried himself like the quarterback Coach Stanley wanted Henry Wallace to become. It's crazy to say that you knew any boy or girl would grow up to become a leader of men and women, but you only had to watch how Jermaine patiently observed you with those clear, slow-blinking eyes to know that one day, he would be followed. We both walked the earth with clenched fists, but Jermaine's fists seemed more likely to open and offer you whatever you needed to get by.

Less than ten years after I visited my cousin in Chicago, Jermaine's little sister was murdered. Months later, Jermaine was incarcerated for manslaughter.

A little over a year ago, Jermaine got off probation, which meant he could finally leave Illinois. After exchanging a few texts about how sure he was Derrick Rose wouldn't let his Bulls fall to LeBron "KANG" James, Jermaine texted me, "Cuzzo I just want to be somewhere where I have some healthy choices. Can you help?" I texted him back, stating that I'd do whatever it took to get him and his little girls to New York so they all could breathe a different kind of air. I meant every word I texted, too.

Jermaine never asked me when he could come to New York. Instead, he sent periodic text messages praising his team, the Bulls, and questioning the bench production of my team, the Heat. "Win or go home, cuzzo" was his favorite text message. I'd get this text whenever his team played a great half or Rose bent laws of physics. Jermaine and I found joy in knowing that black boys from places like Jackson and Chicago were using their athletic genius to obliterate expectations.

That was more than a year ago.

Jermaine is still in Illinois, piecing together work here and there, and I wake up every morning in a world distinguished by rolling hills, manicured meadows, potbellied squirrels, aged gnomes, and a make-out spot called Sunset Lake. Not only have I not sent for Jermaine and his family to join me, I haven't even asked him to come out for a weekend.

The worst of me, I understand, has less power than *the worst of white folks,* but morally is really no better. The worst of me wants credit for intending to do right by Jermaine, and has no intentions of disrupting my life for the needs of a cousin I always looked up to. I am no more equipped to use or understand the language and work of American responsibility as a grown-ass man than I was as a seventh-grader in the halls of Holy Family Catholic School.

A few years after David Rozier indirectly tried to show me the language and work of American responsibility, he and Henry Wallace were dead. The truth is that half the boys in that seventh-grade class at Holy Family died before reaching thirty-five years of age. I used to spend hours daydreaming about David, Henry, Roy Bennett, Tim Brown, Kareem Hill, and Jermaine while playing behind Lerthon's house. Roy, Tim, Kareem, Jermaine, Lerthon and I were teenagers in my dream. David and Henry were not.

***

As our nation shamefully debated Chicago's murder rate during the summer of 2012, folding complicated human lives into convenient numbers that were shared, "liked," discussed, and neglected all around the country, I spent more time talking to Catherine Coleman, my grandmother.

I told her that I might attend this "Peace" basketball tournament in Chicago to promote an end to all the violence. I asked her what she thought of my inviting Jermaine to come with me.

Grandma was quiet for a while. Then she asked me whether the Chicago mothers and grandmothers of kids living and dead would be attending the game.

"I don't know," I told her. "Probably some will."

"Tell those folks at the game that it would help to get the mamas and grandmamas there," she said. "And tell everybody watching them boys play ball that they need to listen to what the mamas and grandmamas have to say."

It made too much sense.

Though my grandmother worked from the time she was seven years old, our nation forbade her from registering to vote until she was deep into her thirties. She has lived under American apartheid longer than she's been technically "free." Our nation told her she would enter the chicken plant as a line worker and retire as a line worker, no matter how well she worked. Our nation limited the amount of formal education she herself could attain and patted her on the back when she earned enough to buy her daughters and son a set of encyclopedias. Our nation watched her raise four black children and two grandchildren to become teachers, all the while responsibly arming herself and her community against *the worst of white folks* and the destructive tendencies of neighbors.

Last month, after burying her brother, Rudy, Grandma bent her knees and reckoned with burying her son, her sisters, her mother, her grandmother, her father, and all four of her best friends. She asked her God to spare her the responsibility of burying any more of her children or grandchildren. A few weeks later, an irresponsible American aspiring to be the leader of our nation, who got a majority of the vote from *the worst of white folks*, called her a "victim" who feels entitled to health care, food, and housing.

Catherine Coleman, along with my Grandma Pudding, and David Rozier's grandmother, have never been allowed to just be victims. They're rarely even allowed to be Americans. They don't get invited to panel discussions. They aren't talked to by the DNC or RNC. No one asks them what to do about national violence, debt, or defense. They are not American super-women, but they are the best of Americans. They have remained responsible, critical, and loving in the face of servitude, sexual assault, segregation, poverty, and psychological violence. They have done this hard, messy work because they were committed to life and justice, and so we all might live more responsibly tomorrow.

There is a price to pay for ducking responsibility, for clinging to the worst of us, for harboring a warped innocence. There is an even greater price to pay for ignoring, demeaning, and unfairly burdening those Americans who have disproportionately borne the weight of American irresponsibility for so long. Our grandmothers and great-grandmothers have paid more than their fair share, and our nation owes them and their children, and their children's children, a lifetime of healthy choices and second chances. That would be responsible.

***

When David Rozier came back to school the day after we were kicked out, he started playing this game where he would fart every time Henry mispronounced "strong" like "skrong," and "straight" like "skraight." David had me dying! I put my head down on my desk so I wouldn't get kicked out of school again and laughed into my forearm until I cried.

At recess, I asked David, "What happened to all that responsibility you were talking about?"

"Oh," he said and took off running a post pattern in the schoolyard. "Nigga, that was yesterday!"

I threw David a bomb, and as the ball half-spiraled through the air, neither one of us thought about tomorrow or yesterday. We were just happy to be in the moment, happy to be alive.

How to Slowly Kill Yourself
and Others in America

I'VE HAD GUNS PULLED ON ME BY FOUR PEOPLE under Central Mississippi skies—once by a white undercover cop, once by a young brother trying to rob me for the leftovers of a weak work-study check, once by my mother, and twice by myself. Not sure how or if I've helped many folks say yes to life, but I've definitely aided in a few folks dying slowly in America, all without the aid of a gun.

***

I'm seventeen, five years younger than Rekia Boyd will be when she is shot in the head by an off-duty police officer in Chicago in 2012. It's the summer after I graduated high school and my teammate, Troy, is back in Jackson, Mississippi. Troy, who plays college ball in Florida, asks me if I want to go to McDonald's on I-55.

As Troy, Cleta, Leighton, and I walk out of McDonald's, I hold the door for open for a tiny, scruffy-faced white man with a green John Deere hat on.

"Thanks, partner," he says.

A few minutes later, we're driving down I-55 when John Deere drives up and lowers his window. I figure that he wants to say something funny since we'd had a cordial moment at McDonald's.

As soon as I roll my window down, the man screams, "Nigger lovers!" and speeds off.

On I-55, we pull up beside John Deere and I'm throwing finger-signs, calling John Deere all kinds of clever "motherfuckers." The dude slows down and gets behind us. I turn around, hoping he pulls over.

Nope.

John Deere pulls out a police siren and places it on top of his car. Troy is cussing my ass out and frantically trying to drive his mama's Lincoln away from John Deere. My heart is pounding out of my chest—not out of fear, but because I want a chance to choke the shit out of John Deere. I can't think of any other way of making him feel what we felt.

Troy drives into his apartment complex and parks his mama's long Lincoln under some kind of shed. Everyone in the car is slumped down at this point. Around twenty seconds after we park, here comes the red, white, and blue of the siren.

We hear a car door slam, then a loud knock on the back window. John Deere has a gun in one hand and a badge in the other. He's telling me to get out of the car. My lips still smell like Filet-O-Fish.

"Only you," he says to me. "You going to jail tonight." He's got the gun to my chest.

"Fuck you," I tell him and suck my teeth. "I ain't going nowhere."

I don't know what's wrong with me.

Cleta is up front trying to reason with the man through her window when all of a sudden, in a scene straight out of *Boyz N the Hood*, a black cop approaches the car and accuses us of doing something wrong. Minutes later, a white cop tells us that John Deere has been drinking too much, and he lets us go.

Sixteen months later, I'm eighteen, three years older than Edward Evans will be when he is shot in the head behind an abandoned home in Jackson in 2012.

Shonda and I are walking from Subway back to Millsaps College with two of her white friends. It's nighttime. We turn off of North State Street and walk halfway past the cemetery when a red Corolla filled with black boys stops in front of us. All of the boys have blue rags covering their noses and mouths. One of the boys, a kid at least two years younger than me with the birdest of bird chests, gets out of the car clutching a shiny silver gun.

He comes toward Shonda and me.

"Me," I say to him. "Me. Me." I hold my hands up, encouraging him to do whatever he needs to do. If he shoots me, well, I guess bullets enter and hopefully exit my chest, but if he thinks I'm getting pistol-whupped in front of a cemetery and my girlfriend off of State Street, I'm convinced I'm going to take the gun and beat him into a burnt cinnamon roll.

The boy places his gun on my chest and keeps looking back and forth to the car.

I feel a strange calm, an uncanny resolve. I don't know what's wrong with me. He's patting me down for money that I don't have, since we hadn't gotten our work-study checks yet and I had just spent my last little money on two turkey subs and two of those large chocolate chip cookies.

The young brother keeps looking back to the car, unsure what he's supposed to do. Shonda and her friends are screaming when he takes the gun off my chest and trots goofily back to the car.

I don't know what's wrong with him, but a few months later, I have a gun.

A partner of mine hooks me up with a partner of his who lets me hold something. I get the gun not just to defend myself from goofy brothers in red Corollas trying to rob folks for work-study money. I guess I'm working on becoming a black writer in Mississippi and some folks around Millsaps College don't like the essays I'm writing in the school newspaper.

A few weeks earlier, George Harmon, the president of Millsaps, shuts down the campus paper in response to a satirical essay I wrote on communal masturbation and sends a letter to more than 12,000 overwhelmingly white Millsaps students, friends, and alumnae. The letter states that the "key essay in question was written by Kiese Laymon, a controversial writer who consistently editorializes on race issues."

After the president's letter goes out, my life kinda hurts.

I receive a sweet letter in the mail with the burnt-up ashes of my essays. The letter says that if I don't stop writing and give myself "over to right," my life will end up like the ashes of my writing.

The tires of my mama's car are slashed when it was left on campus. I'm given a single room after the dean of students thinks it's too dangerous for me to have a roommate. Finally, Greg Miller, an English professor, writes a supportive essay about how and why a student in his Liberal Studies class says, "Kiese should be killed for what he's writing." I feel a lot when I read those words, but mainly I wonder what's wrong with me.

It's Bid Day at Millsaps.

Shonda and I are headed to our jobs at Ton-o-Fun, a fake-ass Chuck E. Cheese behind Northpark Mall. We're wearing royal blue shirts with a strange smiling animal and "Ton-o-Fun" on the left titty. The shirts of the other boy workers at Ton-o-Fun fit them better than mine fit me. My shirt is tight in the wrong places and slightly less royal blue. I like to add a taste of bleach so I don't stank.

As we walk out to the parking lot of my dorm, the Kappa Alpha and Kappa Sigma fraternities are in front of the dorm receiving their new members. They've been up drinking all night. Some of them have on black face and others have on Afro wigs and Confederate capes.

We get close to Shonda's Saturn and one of the men says, "Kiese, write about this!" Then another voice calls me a "nigger" and Shonda a "nigger bitch." I think and feel a lot but mostly I feel that I can't do anything to make the boys feel like they've made us feel right there, so I go back to my dorm room to get something.

On the way there, Shonda picks up a glass bottle out of the trash. I tell her to wait outside the room. I open the bottom drawer and look at the hoodies balled up on top of my gun. I pick up my gun and think about my grandma. I think not only about what she'd feel if I went back out there with a gun. I think about how if Grandma walked out of that room with a gun in hand, she'd use it. No question.

I am her grandson.

I throw the gun back on top of the clothes, close the drawer, go in my closet, and pick up a wooden T-ball bat.

Some of the KAs and Sigs keep calling us names as we approach them. I step, throw down the bat, and tell them I don't need a bat to fuck them up. I don't know what's wrong with me. My fists are balled up and the only thing I want in the world is to swing back over and over again. Shonda feels the same, I think. She's right in the mix, yelling, crying, fighting as best she can. After security and a dean break up the mess, the frats go back to receiving their new pledges and Shonda and I go to work at Ton-o-Fun in our dirty blue shirts. We wonder if this is just kids being kids.

I stank.

On our first break at work, we decide that we should call a local news station so the rest of Jackson can see what's happening at Millsaps on a Saturday morning. We meet the camera crew at school. Some of boys go after the reporter and cameraman. The camera gets a few students in Afros, black face, and Confederate capes. They also get footage of "another altercation."

A few weeks pass and George Harmon, the president of the college, doesn't like that this footage of his college is now on television and in newspapers all across the country. The college decides that two individual fraternity members, Shonda, and I will be put on disciplinary probation for using "racially insensitive language" and that the two fraternities involved get their party privileges taken away for a semester. If there was racially insensitive language Shonda and I could have used to make those boys feel like we felt, we would have never stepped to them in the first place. Millsaps is trying to prove to the nation that it is a post-race(ist) institution and to its alums that all the Bid Day stuff is the work of an "adroit entrepreneur of racial conflict," as I am called in a letter to the editor in the *Clarion Ledger*.

A few months later, Mama and I sit in President George Harmon's office. The table is an oblong mix of mahogany and ice water. All the men at the table are smiling, flipping through papers, and twirling pens in their hands except for me. I am still nineteen, four years older than Hadiya Pendleton will be when she is murdered in Chicago.

President Harmon and his lawyers don't look me in the eye. They zero in on the eyes of Mama, as Harmon tells her that I am being suspended from Millsaps for at least a year for taking and returning *The Red Badge of Courage* from the library without formally checking it out.

He ain't lying.

I took the book out of the library for Shonda's brother without checking it out and I returned it the next day. I looked right at the camera when I did it, too. I did all of this knowing I was on parole, but not believing any college in America, even one in Mississippi, would kick a student out for a year for taking and returning a library book without properly checking it out.

I should have believed.

George Harmon tells me, while looking at my mother, that I will be allowed to come back to Millsaps College in a year only after having attended therapy sessions for racial insensitivity. We are told he has given my writing to a local psychologist and the shrink believes I need help. Even if I am admitted back as a student, I will remain formally on parole for the rest of my undergrad career, which means that I will be expelled from Millsaps College unless I'm perfect.

Nineteen-year-old black boys cannot be perfect in America. Neither can sixty-year-old white boys named George.

Before riding home with Mama, I go to my room, put the gun in my backpack, and get in her car.

On the way home, Mama stops by the zoo to talk about what just happened in George Harmon's office. She's crying and asking me over and over again why I took and returned the gotdamn book knowing they were watching me. Like a loving black mother of her only black boy, Mama starts blaming Shonda for asking me to check the book out in the first place. I don't know what to say other than that I knew it wasn't Shonda's fault and that I left my ID behind and I didn't want to swing back to get it, so I keep walking and say nothing. She says that Grandma is going to be so disappointed in me.

"Heartbroken" is the word she uses.

There.

I feel this toxic miasma unlike anything I've ever felt, not just in my body, but in my blood. I remember the wobbly way my grandma twitches her eyes at my Uncle Jimmy and I imagine being at the end of that twitch for the rest of my life. For the first time in almost two years, I hide my face, grit my crooked teeth, and sob.

I don't stop for weeks.

The NAACP and lawyers get involved in filing a lawsuit against Millsaps on my behalf. Whenever the NAACP folks talk to me or to the newspaper, they talk about how ironic it is that a black boy trying to read a book gets kicked out of college. I appreciate their work, but I don't think the irony lies where they think it does. If I'd never read a book in my life, I shouldn't have been punished that way for taking and bringing back a library book—not when kids are smoking that good stuff, drinking themselves unconscious, and doing some of everything imaginable to nonconsenting bodies.

That's what I tell all the newspapers and television reporters who ask. To my friends, I say that after stealing all those Lucky Charms, Funyons, loaves of light bread, and over a hundred cold dranks out of the cafeteria in two years, how in the fuck do I get suspended for taking and returning the gotdamn *Red Badge of Courage?*

The day I'm awarded the Benjamin Brown Award, named after a twenty-one-year-old truck driver shot in the back by police officers during a student protest near Jackson State in 1967, I take the bullets out of my gun, throw it in the Ross Barnett Reservoir, and avoid my grandma for a long, long time.

I enroll at Jackson State University, where my mother teaches political science, in the spring semester. Even though I'm not really living at home, Mama and I fight every day over my job at Cutco and her staying with her boyfriend and her not letting me use the car to get to my second job at an HIV hospice since my license is suspended.

Really, we're fighting because she raised me to never ever forget I was born on parole, which means no black hoodies in wrong neighborhoods, no jogging at night, hands in plain sight at all times in public, no intimate relationships with white women, never driving over the speed limit or doing those rolling stops at stop signs, always speaking the King's English in the presence of white folks, never being outperformed in school or in public by white students, and, most importantly, always remembering that no matter what, *the worst of white folks* will do anything to get you.

Mama's antidote to being born a black boy on parole in Central Mississippi is not for us to seek freedom, but to insist on excellence at all times. Mama takes it personal when she realizes that I realize she is wrong. There ain't no antidote to life, I tell her. How free can you be if you really accept that white folks are the traffic cops of your life? Mama tells me that she is not talking about freedom. She says that she is talking about survival.

One blue night Mama tells me that I need to type the rest of my application to Oberlin College after I've already handwritten the personal essay. I tell her that it doesn't matter whether I type it or not since Millsaps is sending a dean's report attached to my transcript. I say some other truthful things I should never say to my mother. Mama goes into her room, lifts up her pillow, and comes out with her gun.

It's raggedy, small, heavy, and black, like an old dead crow. I'd held it a few times before with Mama hiding behind me and a friend of hers around the corner.

Mama points the gun at me and tells me to get the fuck out of her house. I look right at the muzzle pointed at my face and smile the same way I did at the library camera at Millsaps. I don't know what's wrong with me.

"You gonna pull a gun on me over some college application?" I ask her.

"You don't listen until it's too late," she tells me. "Get out of my house and don't ever come back."

I leave the house chuckling, shaking my head, cussing under my breath. I go sit in a shallow ditch. Outside, I wander in the topsy-turvy understanding that Mama's life does not revolve around me and that I'm not doing anything to make her life more joyful, spacious, or happy. I'm an ungrateful burden, an obese weight on her already terrifying life. I sit there in the ditch, knowing that other things are happening in my mother's life, but also knowing that Mama never imagined needing to pull a gun on the child she carried on her back as a sophomore at Jackson State. I'm playing with pine needles, wishing I had headphones—but mostly I'm regretting throwing my gun into the reservoir.

When Mama leaves for work in the morning, I break back into her house, go under her pillow, and get her gun. Mama and I haven't paid the phone or the light bill so it's dark, hot, and lonely in that house, even in the morning. I lie in a bathtub of cold water, still sweating and singing love songs to myself.

I put the gun to my head and cock it.

I think of my grandma and remember that old feeling of being so in love that nothing matters except seeing and being seen by her. I drop the gun to my chest. I'm so sad and I can't really see a way out of what I'm feeling but I'm leaning on memory for help. Faster. Slower. I think I want to hurt myself more than I'm already hurting. I'm not the smartest boy in the world by a long shot, but even in my funk I know that easy remedies like eating your way out of sad, or fucking your way out of sad, or lying your way out of sad, or slanging your way out of sad, or robbing your way out of sad, or gambling your way out of sad, or shooting your way out of sad, are just slower, more acceptable ways for desperate folks, and especially paroled black boys in our country, to kill ourselves and others close to us in America.

I start to spend more time at home over the next few weeks since Mama is out of town with her boyfriend. Mama and I still haven't paid the phone bill, so I'm running down to the pay phone every day, calling one of the admissions counselors at Oberlin College. He won't tell me whether they'll accept me or not, but he does say that Oberlin might want me because of, not in spite of, what happened at Millsaps.

A month passes and I haven't heard from Oberlin. I'm eating too much and dry-humping a woman just as desperate as me, and lying like it's my first job, and daring people to fuck with me more than I have in a long time. I'm writing lots of words, too, but I'm not reckoning. I'm wasting ink on bullshit political analysis and short stories and vacant poems that I never imagine being read or felt by anyone like me. I'm an imitator, not a writer, and really, I'm a waste of writing's time.

The only really joyful times in life come from playing basketball and talking shit with O.G. Raymond "Gunn" Murph, my best friend. Gunn is trying to stop himself from slowly killing himself and others, after a smoldering breakup with V., his girlfriend of eight years. Some days, Gunn and I save each other's lives just by telling and listening to each other's odd-shaped truths.

One black night, Ray is destroying me in Madden and talking all that shit when we hear a woman moaning for help outside of his apartment on Capitol Street. We go downstairs and find a naked woman with open wounds, blood, and bruises all over her black body. She can barely walk or talk through shivering teeth, but we ask her if she wants to come upstairs while we call the ambulance. Gunn and I have taken no sexual assault classes and we listen to way too much "The Diary" and "Ready to Die," but right there, we know not to get too close to the woman and just let her know we're there to do whatever she needs.

She slowly makes her way into the apartment because she's afraid the men might come back. Blood is gushing down the back of her thighs and her scalp. She tells us the three men had one gun. When she makes it up to the apartment, we give the woman a brown towel to sit on and something to wrap herself in. Blood seeps through both and even though she looks so scared and hurt, she also looks so embarrassed. Gunn keeps saying things like, "It's gonna be okay, sweetheart," and I just sit there weakly nodding my head, running from her eyes and getting her more glasses of water. When Gunn goes in his room to take his gun out of his waistband, I look at her and know that no one man could have done this much damage to another human being.

That's what I need to tell myself.

Eventually, the ambulance and police arrive. They ask her a lot of questions and keep looking at us. She tells them that we helped her after she was beaten and raped by three black men in a Monte Carlo. One of the men, she tells the police, was her boyfriend. She refuses to say his name to the police. Gunn looks at me and drops his eyes. Without saying anything, we know that whatever is in the boys in that car has to also be in us. We know that whatever is encouraging them to kill themselves slowly by knowingly mangling the body and spirit of this shivering black girl, is probably the most powerful thing in our lives. We also wonder if whatever is in us that has been slowly encouraging us to kill ourselves is also in the heart and mind of the black girl on the couch.

A few weeks later, I get a letter saying I've been accepted to Oberlin College and they're giving me a boatload of financial aid. Gunn agrees to drive me up to Oberlin and I feel like the luckiest boy on earth—not because I got into Oberlin, but because I survived long enough to remember to say "yes" to life and "no" or at least "slow down" to slow death.

My saying yes to life meant accepting the beauty of growing up black, on parole, surrounded by a family of weird women warriors in Mississippi. It also meant accepting that George Harmon, parts of Millsaps College, parts of my state, much of my country, my heart, and mostly my own reflection, had beaten the dog shit out of me. I still don't know what all this means but I know it's true.

This isn't an essay or a woe-is-we narrative about how hard it is to be a black boy in America. This is a lame attempt at remembering the contours of slow death and life in America for one black American teenager under Central Mississippi skies. I wish I could get my Yoda on right now and sift all this into a clean sociopolitical pull-quote that shows supreme knowledge and absolute emotional transformation, but I don't want to lie.

I want to say that remembering starts not with predictable punditry, or bullshit blogs, or slick art that really asks nothing of us; I want to say that it starts with all of us willing ourselves to remember, tell, and accept those complicated, muffled truths of our lives and deaths, and the lives and deaths of folks all around us over and over again.

Then I want to say that I am who my grandma and Aunt Sue think I am.

I am not.

I'm a walking regret, a truth-teller, a liar, a survivor, a frowning ellipsis, a witness, a dreamer, a teacher, a student, a failure, a joker, a writer whose eyes stay red, and I'm a child of this nation.

I know that as I got deeper into my late twenties, and then my thirties, I managed to continue killing myself and other folks who loved me in spite of me. I know that I've been slowly killed by folks who were as feverishly in need of life and death as I am. The really confusing part is that a few of those folks who have nudged me closer to slow death have also helped me say yes to life when I most needed it. Usually, I didn't accept it. Lots of times, we've taken turns killing ourselves slowly, before trying to bring each other back to life. Maybe that's the necessary stank of love, or maybe — like Frank Ocean says — it's all just bad religion, just tasty watered-down cyanide in a Styrofoam cup.

I don't even know.

I know that by the time I left Mississippi, I was twenty years old, three years older than Trayvon Martin will be when he is murdered for wearing a hoodie and swinging back in the wrong American neighborhood. Four months after I leave Mississippi, San Berry, a twenty-year-old partner of mine who went to Millsaps College with Gunn and me, will be convicted for taking Pam McGill, an amazing social worker, into the woods and shooting her in the head.

San confesses to kidnapping Ms. McGill, driving her to some woods, making her fall to her knees, and pulling the trigger while a seventeen-year-old black boy named Azikiwe waits for him in the car. San will eventually say that Azikiwe encouraged him to do it. Even today, journalists, activists, and others folks in Mississippi wonder what really happened with San, Azikiwe, and Pam McGill that day. Was San trying to swing back? Swinging back at what? Were there mental health issues left unattended? Had Ms. McGill, San, and Azikiwe talked to each other before the day? Why was Azikiwe left in the car when the murder took place? How could someone as committed to people as Pam McGill die so violently? Was the eventual pardon of Azikiwe an act of justice?

I can't front, though. I don't wonder about any of that. Not today.

I wonder what all three of those children of our nation really remember about how to slowly kill themselves and other folks in America the day before parts of them died under the blue-black sky in Central Mississippi.

Our Kind of Ridiculous

WHEN I WAS TWENTY-FOUR, I FLEW PAPER airplanes past the apartment of a thirty-two-year-old white boy named Kurt in Emmaus, Pennsylvania. Kurt rocked a greasy brown mullet, bragged about ironing his bleached Lee's, and said the word "youse" a lot. Even with caked-up cornbread sealing the cracks of his teeth and a raggedy mustache that looked like it was colored by a hyper six-year-old, Kurt always reminded me of somebody cute.

Kurt, whose apartment was directly above mine, lived with two women. One was his girlfriend. She could see. One was his wife. She could not.

Three little boys lived in the apartment with Kurt and his two partners. The youngest boy was Kurt's girlfriend's child. This miniature Viking loved to run his muddy hands through his blond hair and grin when he wasn't growling. The other two boys looked like they rolled around naked in a tub of melted Tootsie Rolls before coming out to play.

I was in Pennsylvania working on my graduate thesis while Nicole, my girlfriend at the time, interned at Rodale Press. Though I had spent most of my life in Mississippi close to black folks who were thirty cents away from a quarter, that summer in Emmaus,

Pennsylvania, was the most intimate I'd ever been with white folks who barely had a pot to piss in.

After paying our rent, food, and utilities, Nicole and I had about $140 left in disposable income every month.

That $140 had me feeling quite bougie.

It was the first summer I hadn't worked as a phone book delivery man, a waiter at Ton-o-Fun, a health care assistant at Grace House, a knife salesman at Cutco, a bootleg porter at the Buie House, a counselor at Upward Bound, or a summer school teacher at Indiana University. I was on a fellowship, which meant for the first time in my life, my job was simply to collect a small check in exchange for not wasting reading's and writing's time.

During the day, when I wasn't reading and writing, I made paper airplanes and talked outside with Shay, our eight-year-old neighbor; Barry, her six-year-old brother; and Kurt's kids. For most of the summer, Kurt's kids looked into our empty apartment through a huge sliding glass door. At first, they would stand about a foot from the door, looking directly at their reflections and our empty living room. A week or so into the summer, all three of Kurt's kids started smashing their faces against the door and running their muddy hands up and down the glass.

Shay and Barry had what Grandma called good home-training. They simply watched Kurt's kids watch us from a distance and whispered in each other's ears.

Our apartment held one chair, one desk, a blow-up bed, a fridge covered in word magnets, and a cranky Mac. While Kurt's place smelled like fried meats, thin gravy, sticky fruit punches, and nappy carpet that rarely got vacuumed, our place smelled like new paint and feet. *Miseducation, ATLiens, Aquemini,* and the greatest hits of Joni Mitchell and Curtis Mayfield worked to shield our ears from Kurt's mash-up of Zeppelin, short-people screams, laughter, and that gotdamn Cartoon Network.

One July weekend, someone got shot in the building next to ours. As soon as the police left, Kurt and I walked over to see what we could.

As we walked, Kurt asked me how to pronounce my name. He'd heard his kids call me "Keith" and Nicole call me "Key" or "Kiese."

After I told him that Keith was fine, he asked me if he could borrow ten dollars. I told him I'd give it to him when we got back to our building.

Kurt and I kept walking and talking about his odd family arrangement and money a little while longer before he asked me if people got shot a lot where I was from.

I stopped to look him in the eye and see if he was asking a question he really wanted answered.

He wouldn't look back.

I didn't tell Kurt anything about missing Mississippi, or how I was reckoning with the fact that a friend of mine had taken a young woman into the Central Mississippi woods, blown her brains out, and was now serving a life sentence. I ignored Kurt's question completely and asked him about Pennsylvania amusement parks, Italian ices, and when he planned on getting a job.

After he answered all my questions, Kurt got really close to my face. He looked up at me and didn't run from my eyes. "Keith, youse should move here," he said. "I'm serious. Youse are different. Youse ain't like your kind."

He kept saying it too, absolutely sure he'd given me that *gift* that a number of white folks I'd met loved to give black folks at the strangest times, the *gift* of being decidedly different than all them other niggers. It felt like Kurt wanted a pat on the back for not saying the word "nigger," two pats for distinguishing one nigger from another nigger, and three pats for inching closer to the realization that black Americans were never niggers to begin with.

On the way back from the murder site, Kurt walked ahead of me. I gripped his bony shoulder before we got to the hill leading up to our building. I asked him if his greasy mullet, his two in-house partners, his caved-in chest, his white BeBe's kids, and his belief in niggers made him different than his kind.

"I ain't racist, Keith," he kept saying.

"That's sweet," I told him.

Kurt wiggled free of my grip and walked up the hill to our building. I caught up with him outside of our glass door. I told him that the problem was that the niggers he believed in knew so much more about his kind than even he did, and that the niggers he believed in were taught to never ever be surprised by the slick shit that came out of the mouths of white folks. Then I got all graduate school on him and spouted some mess about dissonance, dissemblance, white absolution, and how it might be impossible for him to know if I was different than my kind if he didn't know himself.

Kurt turned his back on me and my big words.

He walked upstairs to his family and slammed his door. I walked into our empty apartment, partly disappointed that I didn't slap the taste out of Kurt's mouth and mostly ashamed that there was so much more I wanted to say to him.

If white American entitlement meant anything, it meant that no matter how patronizing, unashamed, deliberate, unintentional, poor, rich, rural, urban, ignorant, and destructive white Americans were, black Americans were still encouraged to work for them, write to them, listen to them, talk with them, run from them, emulate them, teach them, dodge them, and ultimately thank them for not being as fucked up as they could be.

That's part of what I learned in Emmaus, Pennsylvania.

Kurt avoided me the rest of the summer, but his kids still banged their muddy hands on our sliding glass door every morning. A few days after Kurt said I was different than my kind, his youngest child walked into our apartment and started playing with the word magnets on our refrigerator. I placed the words "wash" "your" "dirty" "face" "and" "hands" "sometimes" "boy" in a line and asked him to read that sentence.

Kurt's son looked at the words, moved them around, smiled, and clapped his muddy hands like he was lightweight touched before proudly saying, "Nope. I can't even read, Keith. Nope. I can't. I can't even read!" The little muddy joker said it the way you would expect a white child to say, "Gee! I found the treasure. Yep! I really found the treasure."

I laughed in that child's face for a good minute and a half.

Deep. Terrible. Evil. Sad laughs.

And he laughed back, thinking I was laughing with him.

For worse—never better—nothing I saw, or heard, or smelled, or touched, or felt from Kurt and his family surprised me that summer.

I can't say the same thing about myself.

A month or so after I laughed at that little boy's illiteracy, two of Nicole's friends came to visit. I don't remember much about Nicole's friends except one of them was the roundest short adult I'd ever met and she tried too hard not to sound like she was from rural West Virginia. Every few seconds, she managed to throw the words "ridiculous" and "totally" into something that wasn't ridiculous or totally anything.

Nicole drove a tiny green Geo Metro that I couldn't drive because it was a stick, and also because my license was suspended. The four of us piled in that Geo and headed to a Lilith Fair concert in Hershey. The concert wasn't Fresh Fest, and I didn't love the wet fog of patchouli and weed, or the lack of my kind at the show, but it ended up making me smile and feel a lot.

After the concert, we stopped at a gas station before leaving Hershey and heading back to Emmaus. A few minutes after we got on the interstate, I reminded Nicole to turn on her headlights.

Seconds later, we heard the siren.

A young white cop came to Nicole's side and pointed his flashlight at me in the passenger seat. I asked him if I could open the glove compartment to get her registration. He told me to keep my hands in plain sight.

I laughed at him. "See?" I said to Nicole.

An older white cop came up from behind us and approached my side. Both cops walked to the front of the Geo, talked for a second, then told me to get out of the car.

"For what?" I asked, now fake-laughing.

"Because we saw you throw crack out of the window."

I sucked my teeth. "I'ont even drink," I stupidly told the cop.

I pointed toward the field and told both cops again that I didn't throw shit out of the car and that we could all go look if they wanted to.

When I raised my arms, the bigger cop put his hands on his gun and told me to put my hands on the car. He patted me down and handcuffed me while Nicole watched from the driver's side and her ridiculous round friend sat quietly in the back of the car talking to the girl whose voice I can't even remember.

Blackness is probable cause, I tell myself.

They got me.

I'm standing handcuffed in front of the flashing blue lights of a parked police car and a green Geo Metro. I've had guns pulled on me before and I was never afraid.

This is different.

The handcuffs hurt more than the thought of bullets. The two cops with deep frown lines place me in the back of the police car "for my own good" as a parade of mostly drunk white folks, on their way home from Lilith Fair, drive down the highway looking in our direction.

Shame.

I am guilty of being too much like my kind, which means I am one mistaken movement from being a justifiable homicide, or a few planted rocks from being incarcerated.

This is American law. In Hershey. In Jackson. In Compton. In Oakland. In Brooklyn.

This is American life.

I'm wondering what will happen if I ask the cops, "Do y'all still drink Kool-Aid? Does it make your tongue purple? Remember Tang? Would you ever want us to do this to you and your kids? I'm serious. Don't you think police, teachers, doctors, and dentists should be more just and compassionate than the rest of us? Who protects us from you?"

I'm wondering if Nicole, who is now standing at the back of her green Geo Metro talking to one of the cops, will think I could have actually thrown drugs out of her passenger-side window. This, I tell myself, is why Mama and Grandma got so mad when Nicole's white stepfather disowned her for talking to me. Grandma and Mama believed that if anyone should have used disowning as a tactic to protect their child, it should have been them. But they never did. They never would. They simply said, "Don't get caught riding in the car with white girls" in the same speech during which they told me, "Don't fuck anyone you can't imagine raising a child with."

I'm wondering if Nicole is wondering if she ever really knew me. I'm thinking I should have asked myself that question long before we decided to move in together. I feel so typical.

From the backseat of the police car, I'm watching this blinking blue field where my kind has thrown lots of invisible, and not so invisible, rocks of crack cocaine. I convince myself that Mississippi is on the other side of that field.

I want to run home.

For a second, though—truth be told—I'm wondering if I actually did throw rocks out of the window. Sitting in the back of that police car in handcuffs that had been wrapped around the wrists of many of my kind, I'm wondering if there's any chance that I am what, not who, they think I am.

I'm watching the police search Nicole's car. They pull out my backpack from the trunk. The older cop reaches in the bag and pulls out what looks like some condoms they gave out at Lilith Fair. He holds the backpack up in Nicole's face and shakes his head. He comes to the back of the police car I'm sitting in and tells me to get out.

"Thought you said we wouldn't find anything in your bag," he says.

I get it. This isn't just about race or love; it's mostly about fucking.

As calm as I can, still water cradling my eyes, I say, "You should find that crack you saw me throw or you should let me go." The cop makes some comment about my mouth and takes the handcuffs off.

I don't feel free. I want to run home.

"All the people that you could've stopped, and you chose us?" I say with my hands pressed against my thighs. Cars filled with white folks keep passing us. They're all watching, mostly knowing what my kind is capable of. I wonder if Kurt is in one of those cars. I wonder, too, how many of my kind saw me handcuffed on the side of the road that night.

They want to help, I tell myself. But they already know.

"You'uns safe tonight," the older officer says. "We're just doing our job."

They still got us, I tell myself. They still got us.

"That was so ridiculous," Nicole's friend keeps saying from the backseat as we head home. "That was so totally ridiculous."

No one else is saying a word. Nicole is driving eight miles per hour below the speed limit.

As we get closer to Emmaus, Nicole's friend starts replaying what happened from the beginning of the concert to the cops saying I threw crack out the window.

She nervously says "totally" and "ridiculous" a few more times. She never says "afraid," "angry," "worried," "complicit," "tired," or "ashamed."

We got out of the Geo and saw the blue flickering of the TV on the upstairs balcony of Kurt's apartment. Kurt and his family were watching something with a loud laugh track. Our sliding glass door was covered in new muddy smudges.

I walked into the smaller bedroom of our apartment. While Nicole's friend kept replaying what happened for the third time in the living room, I dug my feet into the carpet of the bedroom and tried to push myself through the wall.

Nicole knocked on the door.

"You OK?" she asked me.

"I'm good," I said. "For real. You should spend some time with your friends before they leave."

Nicole looked at me like she wanted to say everything was going to be okay. I wanted her to say that we were the collateral damage of a nation going through growing pains. Part of me wanted us to hug and agree each other to death that we were better people than we actually were. But most of me was tired of lying to myself and really tired of talking to white folks.

Nicole kept staring at me through the silence when we heard some thumping and screaming upstairs. I told her that I was sorry for being a dick, but I just wanted to read and write before going to bed.

I grabbed my notebook and told myself I was going to use that day as fuel to finish a chapter I was writing about four kids from Mississippi who time-travel through a hole in the ground. The kids think time-travel is the only way to make their state and their nation love itself and the kids coming after them. I scribbled away at a chapter before getting stuck on these two sentences one of the characters sees written in sawdust in a workshed around 1964:

> *We are real black characters with real character, not the stars of American racist spectacle. Blackness is not probable cause.*

> *We are real black characters with real character, not the stars of American racist spectacle. Blackness is not probable cause.*

> *We are real black characters with real character, not the stars of American racist spectacle. Blackness is not probable cause.*

> *We are real black characters...*

After what happened that day, all that really mattered was making it to those two clunky sentences. Everything else, including Kurt's intentions, Nicole's nervous friend, and my shame at getting niggered by two perverted police officers, was as light as the paper airplanes I threw past Kurt's apartment. And making it to that point, as quiet as it's kept, felt like the most that one of my kind could ask for, especially a few minutes from some invisible crack, not that many miles from Mississippi, and directly beneath the apartment of an American white boy who needed to say "youse" and "your kind" way more than some of y'all could ever imagine.

Hip-Hop Stole My Southern Black Boy

IN 1998, I STOOD IN THE BASEMENT BATHROOM OF Mudd Library at Oberlin College and asked myself, *Quick, Kie, what in the hell is a cipher?* It was a question I couldn't ask out loud, as I was speaking of the word, not *Tha Cypher*, a magazine that Rich Santiago, from the Bronx, and David Jacobs were creating outside the bathroom. The word "cipher," I remembered had initially crept up on me in a much smaller Central Mississippi bathroom back in 1992.

Back then, fifteen minutes into our lunch period, seven of us descended into what we called the B-Boy bathroom. B-Boy for us meant neither Breaker Boy, Bad Boy, nor Bronx Boy; it meant Black Boy. There, B. Dazzle, who was the little brother of god-emcee Kamikaze of the group Crooked Lettaz, chaired a lyrical demolition of Stacy "King Slender" Hill.

I slouched between two urinals, hands cupped over mouth, providing a weak beat box while B. Dazzle went on and on and on... Every Black Boy in the bathroom caught a vibe from his lyrics, or at least we acted like he did, *in spite* of the fact that we were the Southern Niggas who needed to get wiser, and *because* we were the Southern Niggas who ironically felt wiser and more real just by listening to B. Dazzle. The seven of us, including the just-dissed King Slender, bobbed our heads and pumped our fists like we knew what everything in his rhyme, including his "cipher," really meant.

You had to be a B-Boy to enter our space. No black girls, Asians, or white folks stepped foot in the B-Boy bathroom when we rocked it. In my imagination, I always see K. Parry, a gregarious, theatrical, give-peace-a-chance white guy trying to Rocky his way into our space with some sharp wit and dramatic vocal bombast. This large thespian wobbles into the bathroom in some stone-washed cutoffs and penny loafers. He proceeds to spit a monologue that doesn't even rhyme before getting sliced up by the previously demolished King Slender, who says something like, "...I'm Clubber Lang, K. Parry, not Stacy the Hill/This the Nigga version of Rocky and Balboa gettin' killed." King Slender ends it by saying, "Live on, Apollo Creed."

Classic.

Black girls couldn't be a real part of our space because they were busy with their own rituals. Plus, getting caught in the opposite sex's bathroom got you suspended for a week. We cracked open the door of the bathroom just enough so the black girls could hear. And what they heard, probably more than our actual rhymes, were our responses to our rhymes. As the beat box–accompanied boasts, confessionals, and critiques moved from between urinals and stalls out the door of the bathroom into the hallway, the black girls, white folks, Asians, and wack niggas could only consume and interrogate the sound, not the creative culture or experience from whence that sound sprang. Our cipher was off limits to them, B. Dazzle told me. And quiet as it was kept, we wanted it that way. We wanted the black girls, especially, to need to hear what we were up to from a distance, but we refused to conceive them as our primary audience. Conversely, they kept us out of their private rituals, too.

From our position, the black girls in the hall were positioned in the same way we were positioned as Southern eavesdroppers of New York hip-hop. Some would get close as they could to the crack of the door, but they could never come all the way in. We understood that the seven Southern Black Boys in that space were private, mysterious, and desired by folk who didn't really know how or why we did what we did. That belief made us feel more powerful, possessed, closer to real hip-hop and strangely closer to New York.

Within that B-Boy room, all of us knew that hip-hop credibility had little to do with the quality of your boast, the intensity of your critique, or the passion of your confessional. Really, it was all rooted in your hip-hop aesthetic. And that aesthetic seemed to be rooted in geography. Hip-hop and New York became unspoken adjectives in small Southern spaces like this, and one's worth in the B-Boy room was based almost solely on how hip-hop or New York the other six listeners thought you and your style were.

I had a decent bit of hip-hop credibility due to spending summers in upstate New York visiting my father (to most black Mississippians, New York state meant New York City), but my rhyme style was too deliberate, dirty, local, filled with too many "or" words that were pronounced with a long "o" to be considered authentic New York. "Now I need no mic," I would rap, "just a slow-ass tempo/step to me wrong and motherfucker, you in fo'/a beat down that'll go down in your history books/come try and fuck with Kie, get yo ego took." That was the favorite of my four lyrical styles. And the other three styles, though dope in their own way, sounded remarkably close to that one. In the B-Boy bathroom, my rhymes swayed the crowd, but the movement started and stopped in between those two Central Mississippi urinals. B. Dazzle, on the other hand, moved the crowd to different states, figuratively and literally, and his character was as desired and enigmatic as his rhymes.

I believed the myth was that B. Dazzle and his older brother, Kamikaze, spent summers not in Poughkeepsie, Rochester, Albany, or Syracuse, but at some cousin's place in the South Bronx. The myth allowed me to slavishly follow when B. Dazzle chided us to use the term "hip-hop" instead of "rap," and "cipher" instead of "rap circle." "Hip-hop is more lyrical, more New York, nigga," he told me. He said it was universal, real, filled with brothers in ciphers dropping knowledge, breaking, deejaying, graffiti writing, showing, and proving, while rap music, on the ashy black-hand side, was artistically inferior, country-sounding, and local.

Henry James didn't have to tell us that geography was fate. Shit, we knew that. The seven of us had similar dreams of being divine emcees, too, though we knew geography wouldn't allow it. Plus, our mamas and grandparents had other plans, and they made sure we became multiple dreamers who actualized boring dreams like becoming managers, counterfeiters, computer engineers, racketeers, sergeants, pimps, and college professors.

As much as parts of us tried not to be, we were country Black Boys with little to no experience with real New York hip-hop except *Yo! MTV Raps* and *Rap City,* or when the Fresh Fest came to the Coliseum or KRS-ONE came to Jackson State University. And by Mississippi standards, the seven of us weren't even that country because we were from the city of Jackson. In Jackson, and other parts of the Black Belt, we were no longer the dutiful disciples of the Holy Trinity of MCs—Kane, KRS, and Rakim. We respected the gods, but we were done exclusively eavesdropping on the rhymes coming out of New York City. West Coast music, as varied as it was, met us where we were and, truth be told, it was music we could see and hear. We also accepted that the West Coast and the

Black Belt were family, and had been since the second great migration of the 1940s ushered thousands of southern black families to Los Angeles for jobs in the automotive and defense industries.

It's true that the South, dismissed as culturally slow, meaningless, and less hip (hop) than New York, had yet to, as Albert Murray wrote, lyrically stylize our Southern worlds into significance. But if outsiders really listened to the musty movement behind the Geto Boyz, UGK, Eight Ball, and MJG, they would have heard the din of deeply Southern Black Boys and girls eager to keep it real *local*. We wanted to use hip-hop's brash boast, confessional, and critique to unapologetically order the chaos of our country lives through country lenses, with little regard for whether it sounded like *real* hip-hop.

We were on our way to realizing that we were blues people, familiar in some way or another with dirt. There were no skyscrapers and orange-brown projects stopping us from looking up and out. We didn't know what it was like to move in hordes, with enclosed subway trains slithering beneath our feet.

And we liked it that way.

En route to lyrical acceptance of our dirty, we met Scarface, JT Money, Ice Cube, Bun B, MC Ren, and D.O.C. And after a while, we realized that they were our cousins, our uncles, our best friends, us. We rode through Compton, Oakland, Port Arthur, and Houston the same way we rode through Jackson, Meridian, Little Rock, New Orleans, and Birmingham. We rode in long cars with windows down, bass quaking, and air fresheners sparkling like Christmas tree ornaments.

We felt pride in knowing that the greatest producer alive was an uncle from Compton and the most anticipated emcee in the history of hip-hop was a lanky brother from Long Beach. We knew, no matter what anyone in New York said, that the baddest emcee on earth, song for song, album for album, was an aging cousin from South Central Los Angeles whose government name was O'Shea.

But B. Dazzle, through his lyrics, clothes, sensibility, and utterances of "ciphers" still reveled in being New York hip-hop. And being New York hip-hop trumped being a Southern Black Boy who wondered if New York hip-hop loved him in the early 1990s. Chicago rapper Common Sense rapped in 1994 about faithfully loving HER, a version (or virgin) of pure hip-hop who moved away from New York essence and lost her soul. We could and couldn't relate, because while the last thing on earth we admitted to wanting to be was a woman or a gay man, our love interest, nonetheless was a HE, a him. And though HE was changing, HE was still sadly New York hip-hop. Around our way, his holy local apostle was a gap-toothed brother with skills and chappy lips named B. Dazzle. The booming acoustics of the B-Boy bathroom and the B-Boy imagination were his Mecca, and since this was before the advent of player-hation, I couldn't hate. All I could do was not let on that I was starting to love a kind of hip-hop that loved me back, and try hard as hell to be down.

That was then.

Rewind (or fast-forward) back to my standing in an Oberlin College bathroom in early 1998. While Rich Santiago and D. Jakes were in the A-level of the library trying to find titles for their new hip-hop magazine, Rich looked at me and said, "Yo Kie, what about *Tha Cypher*." And I was on some, "Yeah man. That's it." Now, exactly why I thought *Tha Cypher* was it is where the story gets a bit shameful. At the time, when I heard "cipher," I didn't think of a tight circle of brothers taking turns boasting, critiquing, and confessing themselves into the world over a beat box. The word "cipher" reminded me solely of B. Dazzle and my faulty obsession.

It sounded industrial, sleek, masculine, New York—like if the magazine could speak, through gapped fronts, he would say "I *am* hip-hop, son. Yah mean? What!"

And I guessed that's what Rich and them wanted in a magazine. But honestly, I understood a few hours later that I might have been too country, too dirty, too much of a Black Boy—might have smelled too many boiling chitlins, said "fenda" too many times, got my ass waxed by too many switches off the chinaberry tree, had comfortably ridden in too many pineconed cabs of pickup trucks—to thoroughly understand what a cipher was in 1992 or 1998. When I said "cipher" over and over again in that bathroom, with all its jaggedly dangling connotations, it sounded fake, forced, clean. *Was our Black Boy Central Mississippi space just another cipher?* The more I said the word, the more I felt like Puffy's verse in *Benjamin's*, Michael Jackson's chin, Vanilla Ice's fade, Hype's *Belly* and *Soul Train* post Don Cornelius. I felt like a something, not a somebody, with forced style and suspect substance, a something that would go to all lengths to never acknowledge its dirtiness, a something that created pleasure in aesthetically being the opposite of a Mississippi Black Boy.

Don't get me wrong! In college, like lots of Southern Black Boys, I could bring the ever fake and flexible "Word," "Nam sayin'?" or "Yo, son" where need be. But stripped of the verbal signifiers of hip-hop, I was left kinda naked. I became what I was running from in that Mississippi B-Boy bathroom in 1992, the opposite of NYC B-Boy. I was an unrefined, red-eyed, dirty, Mississippi Black Boy looking for both acceptance and something to resist anywhere I could find it. In 1992, it was B. Dazzle and in 1998, at Oberlin, it was *Tha Cypher*. Both times, the "it" I really wanted to accept, resist, and love was New York hip-hop. But to love and resist New York hip-hop, I had to believe hip-hop and New York were ends in themselves that had little to do with black Southern me.

And this is where it gets tricky, because by 1998 the South completely accepted its dirtiness. When Goodie Mob asked the question on his classic *Soul Food*, "What you niggas know about the Dirty South?" New York hip-hop's honest answer should have been, "Yo, not a gotdamn thing, son. And we ain't really trying to know that country shit, either."

1998 was the year that the Calio Projects of New Orleans met hip-hop. Everything Master P and No Limit put out went gold and platinum. All over the country, people claimed to be "Bout It." UGK, underground Southern glory at its rawest, was about to show Jay Z and the country how to Big Pimp. Outkast was a few years removed from driving a Southernplayeristic Cadillac from Atlanta to space and back with *ATLiens,* and they were about to redefine sonic chemistry with *Aquemini.* Far from crunk, but also far from the clean bounce of Kriss Kross, Goodie Mob released a follow-up to the critically acclaimed *Soul Food* that pronounced they were *Still Standing.*

Inside the library, D. Jakes and Rich were busy trying to create a magazine that mimicked New York hip-hop ciphers, but in the town of Oberlin, Ohio, and nearby cities like Cleveland, Detroit, and St Louis, folks were listening to and loving how Southern Black Boys were redefining hip-hop. Folks in these other cities watched these Southern artists learn what artists west of the Deep South had learned ten years earlier and Midwest artists like Bone learned four years earlier: they understood that imitating and interrogating New York hip-hop was fruitless without applying that imitation and interrogation to one's local culture, one's place. This understanding was at the core of the success of NWA, Bone, and eventually Outkast. As great a moment as this was for the South, was there anyone who thought that Southern hip-hop would move beyond the heights it reached in 1998? How could it?

That was then.

Rewind or fast-forward to 2013. I'm standing in the bathroom of Vassar College, a college sixty-five miles north of New York City. During the last five years, I sold two blues and hip-hop inspired novels and taught four different courses with hip-hop at their center, including one called "Shawn Carter: Autobiography of an Autobiographer." Many of my students are New York-bred lovers of hip-hop. Around five years ago, I noticed that my kids were beginning to wear those white Lance Armstrong-style wristbands that say "I Love Hip-Hop." Their love for hip-hop, interestingly, didn't know what to do with Southern hip-hop or Mississippi. They didn't love the South or Southern hip-hop and they weren't sure that most Southern artists hadn't stylized their Southern worlds into digestible, aesthetically acceptable terms for "real lovers" of New York hip-hop.

They were equally unsure how to deal with the fact that the South began to sell millions more albums and get way more spins than any other region in the country, while newish New York hip-hop created a number of young artists who actually sounded Southern. So many of my students, like many other so-called purists, dismissed Southern hip-hop as ignorant, catchy, pop, hollow, shameful. Most of my students knew, and wanted me to believe, that in addition to white suburbia's uncritical devouring of the music minus culture and the countless emcees pandering to the black girl audience in the hallway and corporate America's glossy detailing of hip-hop, the music was dying because Three-Six Mafia won an Oscar, Trina showed her booty, Mike Jones went platinum, Li'l Jon couldn't rap, and Trinidad James was Trinidad James.

I honestly didn't see any of this coming in that Central Mississippi B-Boy bathroom twenty years ago, but I did understand that loving New York hip-hop wasn't enough. Isolated from caring and curious black girls in the hallway and a destructive white gaze in my Central Mississippi world, I loved New York and New York hip-hop through the likes of Kane, KRS, Rakim, and LL. But even in that safe space, in longing for hip-hop and loving what B. Dazzle represented, I couldn't fully love my Southern self, Southern black girls, or the culture that created us.

The raggedy clinking of this essay should not contradict the fact that we Southern Black Boys and girls owe New York an almost unpayable debt. New York hip-hop literally gave us means to boast, critique, and confess ourselves into a peculiar existence, in ciphers and on the page. And really, it let us love its brilliance. For that, I will always respect New York ciphers, aesthetics, and sounds.

It's taken me twenty years to understand why my uttering and writing the word "cipher" frightened me for so long. The "cipher" reminded me of the Southern Black Boy who longed, like Lil Wayne, Jay Electronica, and J. Cole a few years ago, for an artistic letter of acceptance from New York. Truth be told, the art of Big K.R.I.T, Charlie Braxton, Cassandra Wilson, and Margaret Walker Alexander helped me reckon with a fear that my work would never be significant without a stylization that accommodated what I believed were New York sensibilities. It doesn't make much sense, but it's true.

I now accept the Black Boys, Invisible Men, Native Sons, and Blues People who grandfolked hip-hop into existence. And just like its grandfolks, I also accept that while it's painfully brilliant, innovative, and inspiring at times, hip-hop hasn't come close to meaningfully loving, accepting, and disagreeing with black girls; it's kept their sensibilities, ears, eyes, and voices in the hallway and/or pandered to what we believe is their pussies, instead of asking and imagining what's happening in their ciphers. It also hasn't come close to faithfully disarming and laughing at white gazes. Nor has it even come close to gracefully mediating the space between the urban and the rural, the gaps between poverty and working poor, the difference between new money and wealth. And though it's come closer to realizing and illuminating these relationships in more considerable ways than contemporary literature, punditry, television, movies, or any mass of critical citizenry, it probably never will.

But if it can't do these things, or we can't do these things through hip-hop, from what are we running when we proclaim a love for hip-hop? That's the question. In and out of B-Boy ciphers, Black Boys like me have been asking a music and a so-called culture, as hokey as it sounds, to do the real work of the self, and the soul—really, work that black Southerners have been doing for decades.

We black Southerners, through life, love, and labor, are the generators and architects of American music, narrative, language, capital, and morality. That belongs to us. Take away all those stolen West African girls and boys forced to find an oral culture to express, resist, and signify in the South, and we have no rich American idiom. Erase Nigger Jim from our literary imagination and we have no American story of conflicted movement, place, and moral conundrum. Eliminate the Great Migration of Southern black girls and boys and you have no Los Angeles, Chicago, Detroit, Indianapolis, Cleveland, or New York City. Expunge the sorrow songs, gospel, and blues of the Deep South and we have no rock and roll, rhythm and blues, funk, or hip-hop.

I am a black Southern artist. Our tradition is responsible for me, and I am responsible to it.

When Outkast won the *The Source* magazine's "Best New Artist" award more than ten years ago at the Apollo, New York booed. Andre 3000 addressed the booing of "them closed-minded folks" with the defiant utterance that "the South got something to say and that's all I got to say." Up until this very point, I've agreed with Andre to death and hoped to God he was right. I now know that he was and he wasn't. The South not only has something to say to New York; it has something to say to itself and to the world, and we've been saying it for years, decades, centuries. As hip-hop has grown way bigger than New York, and the new sound and art coming from New York ciphers and writerly circles have become more mimetic and less soulfully significant, New York and the rest of the country now has to listen, take note, and literally emulate us, even if they still don't fully respect or understand from whence we come.

It's okay.

I'm not sure that what Mississippi artists are saying today is the most meaningful work in the world. I know that it is the most meaningful work in *my* world. And without the historic and contemporary sounds, sayings, and doings of Southern Black Boys like Charlie Braxton, K.R.I.T., Kamikaze, Mychal Denzel Smith, Tito Lopez, Skip Coon, Pyinfamous, Banner, Jay Electronica, and 3000, and Southern black girls like Jesmyn Ward, Missy Elliot, Imani Perry, Erykah Badu, Josie Pickens, Nathalie Collier, Beyonce, Jessica Young, Gangsta Boo, Regina Bradley, Josie Duffy, and Natasha Trethewey, hip-hop and American art would be sleek, conventional, heady, pallid, and paltry as the blank piece of paper on the last page of this book, and probably just as hollow as the center of the next cipher.

Shh...listen. Go ahead and listen hard. Can you hear us? Can you see us? Does that look like blue to you?

It don't even matter no more, cousin. We hear us. We hear you, too. Exactly. And that's all I should have ever had to say about that.

Echo: Mychal, Darnell, Kiese, Kai, and Marlon

PEACE FAM,

I'm just waking up on the anniversary of Malcolm X's assassination, the birthday of Nina Simone, and I feel small. I'm not comparing my life's accomplishments to either of them. I've learned enough to stop making that mistake. But I still compare myself to who I think I should be by now and the vision is incomplete.

I'm twenty-six now, and for the first time I feel comfortable enough calling myself a man, but can't help thinking of all the years I was confused about what that meant. I got into an argument with my pops when I was twenty-one, I can't remember what it was about, and he asked me, "Do you think you're a man now?" and through my whimpering I admitted, "No." I was answering on his terms. I was still in school. I didn't have any real bills, or a job, a place of my own...you know, man shit. And the longer I went without any of those things, the less I felt like I would ever become a man, with his eyes constantly on me, asking without saying, "When are you going to get it together?"

Hell if I knew. I had this vague idea about being a writer because that's the only skill I had (still is, but don't sleep on my cookie-baking abilities), with no earthly idea of how to make that happen. The days I didn't have an appointment with my therapist

I spent in bed watching cable news and writing really horrible poetry. When I wasn't having a panic attack, I was thinking about the last panic attack and anticipating the next. All the while, the disappointment in my pops's eyes was palpable. He was wondering where he went wrong and I was being crippled by the thought that I'd never be enough of a man to make him proud.

I'm trying to pinpoint the moment I stopped worrying and started living. I can't, really. I still worry, but it doesn't overwhelm me. Something broke along the way and I'm free. I can call myself a man now because I love and feel loved. And for me that's all it takes.

I think of all the time I wasted not knowing that and I feel small. I'm looking at my text messages now. Yesterday, my pops told me he loved me. I'm twenty-six, he'll be fifty-two soon, and I think he's told me he loves me more in the last year or so than during the entire rest of my life. I can't help but think of what we missed.

I wish I had that time back. I wish I knew my worth a long time ago. But here I am.

With love,
Mychal Denzel Smith

***

DEAR MYCHAL,

I cannot help but think that this performance called "living" is the most radical act that we black men can commit ourselves to.

Unlike you, I did not (and still do not) spend a lot of time in therapy, even though I graduated with a master's degree in clinical counseling, and even though I knew, the first time that I tried to end my life, that I needed help more than the helping profession needed me. But like you, I spent a lot of time in bed during my early twenties. Dreams, when I could actually sleep, were a welcome escape from...

Life: Staying awake, staying alive, meant that I needed to figure out how the hell I would persuade other folks in my life that I was straight and, therefore, acceptable and honorable as a black man. Fuck trying to live for my father, who didn't know that I wanted to die...who didn't know what undergrad institution I was in at the time...who didn't really know me...probably because he too was most likely trying just as hard as me to live. Nah, I was too worried about living for the Father, that other God, who apparently hated me enough to let me burn eternally in hell because I preferred to love other men. Ain't that torture? But my black mama knew best. She told me that I should not keep anyone in my life who refused to love me.

Yet, if I were to adhere to my mom's advice, I would have had to drop out of school years ago (since a lot of folks in our inequitable educational system refuse to love us), quit engaging public health offices (because I walked in as a human in need of medical services and walked out as a patient whose subjective world was made invisible by research lingo: "MSM," otherwise known as "men who have sex with men"), sleep in my bed all damn day (knowing it is more likely that I would be stopped by police when walking to the store in Camden or Bed-Stuy while rocking a fitted cap and carrying books than my white male neighbors would be while walking around in ski masks in the middle of summer and dropping a dime bag on the ground in front of a walking police and his dog)...

See, this thing that we call "living" is as revolutionary as black gay Joseph Beam's call for black men to love other black men, precisely because it is a command for us to counteract the very processes of annihilation that structural racism and patriarchy have taught us to love and replicate. We are experts in the art of killing because we know what it is like to be killed, maligned, have our spirits deadened, our bodies pillaged. We know. But we cannot demonstrate our knowledge by rearticulating the very violences that have been used to murder us.

I am a black man and I am still alive. And, yes, I am a revolutionary, because I daily choose to live! But I am a black man whose black mama's body and spirit were terrorized by another black man's hands and words. *Sexism and patriarchy are not part of the revolution.* I am a gender-maneuvering gay black man whose spirit was terrorized by other straight black men. *Heterosexism and heteronormativity are not a part of our revolution.* I am a black man who has ignored the plights of so many of my brothers. *Separation because of difference and elitism based on class is not a part of the revolution.* Indeed, my living is your living, is your father's living, is my father's living, is my mother's living, is the stranger's living, and it is the revolution.

If God needs to condemn anything to hell, it ought to be the idea of social death. Every day we commit an act of revolution, an act of treason, against a system that was never meant to guarantee our survival.

More love,
Darnell Moore

***

DEAR DARNELL AND MYCHAL,

Your letter to Mychal took me back to a Baldwin essay. In "Alas Poor Richard," an essay that I still find a bit too brutalizing of Richard Wright, Baldwin wrote, "Negroes know about each other what can here be called family secrets, and this means that one Negro, if he wishes can 'knock' the other's 'hustle,' can give his game away."

Long before I read the Baldwin essay, and long before I remember Tupac Shakur, Nasir Jones, and Dwayne Carter giving lessons on how our love for brothers and riches was always more important than our love of black women, I understood the gendered expectation of that hustle Baldwin writes about. No matter what another black man I cared for did to a woman or a group of women or his male partner, I was never to call him out or tell other people about his game.

I want to change.

The black man with whom I spent most of my life was not my father. This black man had an aneurysm two weeks ago. Bad books would call this black man "a father figure." (Like both of you, I try not to write bad books.) This black man never told me he loved me. He never called me his son. He never told me I could be better. And, truth be told, I never wanted or needed him to do any of that shit. I liked him and I think he liked me.

That was enough.

Femiphobic diatribes and other bad books have gassed us with this idea that black boys need the presence of black father figures in our lives. I'm sure I'm not the only black boy who realized a long time ago that my mother and her mother and her mother's mother needed loving, generous partners far more than I needed a present father.

Mama disciplined me. She loved me.

Aunt Sue prayed for me. She loved me.

Grandma worked for me. She loved me.

That's why I made it through the late 80s and 90s. That is why I am alive. Black children need waves of present, multifaceted love, not simply present fathers.

Anyway, I believed this black man loved how my mother made him feel…until he didn't. He loved her mind…until he didn't. He loved her persistence…until he didn't. I know my mother loved him, and loved what he tried to teach me. This black man tried to teach me that white folks were never to be emulated, that black life came from black farmers, and that a love of black people necessitated a love of the land we toiled, picked, and raked. This black man tried to teach me to own myself, Darnell, to never work for a white man. I learned later that owning myself was very different and, really, a lot easier than loving myself.

This black man physically and emotionally brutalized my mother. I fought him for that, but I never told anyone. My mother broke up fights between us. I wiped her tears, put ice on her swollen eyes and split lips, and never ever talked about what this man did to her. This black man was respected in our community and I could have knocked his hustle by telling the truth to him, to my mother, or to anyone who knew us, but I never did.

I knew not to. I knew that telling was not only spreading my mama's business; it was also a form of knocking this black man's hustle. And that, I believed, was not how one black man should love another.

Darnell, your letter really made me think about how not knocking another brother's hustle was seen as black men loving black men. Your letter reminds me that any love that necessitates deception is not love. It doesn't matter if that supposed love is institutional or personal. Your letter reminds me that when you don't let love breathe, you can't be surprised when you and those around you suffocate. We black men have suffocated our partners and ourselves for a long, long time. We black men have been suffocating. For a long, long time. And I'd like it to stop. I want to work on loving you and Mychal and Kai and Marlon, and I want all of you to work on loving me. Please knock my hustle, Darnell. Please remain my friend when I knock yours. Please love me, brother, and encourage me to be a healthy part of healthy relationships, no matter what. There is no proof that most of this nation has ever really wanted us to live with dignity and equal access to healthy choices, so we have to take better care of ourselves. We have to change.

I am regretful and ready to love.

I need your help,
Kiese Laymon

***

DEAR KIESE, DARNELL, AND MYCHAL,

I THANK you.

I THANK you for being vulnerable. I thank you for going deep and being unafraid to share that with me. All of these letters made me ask myself a question that I ponder a lot: What do we do with the scars, those of us who did not die, but still aren't free? We struggle. We fight. We make a way out of no way. Every day we prove that the impossible is possible just by living.

You are right, Mychal, trading worry for living, for being, is freedom—it's about being present.

You are right, Darnell, loving ourselves is a revolutionary act—we have to practice because the preachers and their Bibles don't always tell us so.

You are right, Kiese, love can't be attained through ownership—love is a relationship that must be cultivated through honesty. The truth can hurt, but a lie will never set you free. I, like you, choose truth. Please love me enough to tell me the truth.

Can we heal ourselves?

Yes! And we are modeling that process here. It takes self-reflection.

These days when I look in the mirror, I see change. I see my hips narrowing. I see my jaw-line sharpening. I see the physical markers of black manhood etch a divine design upon my body, and I feel pretty.

But I wasn't born this way. I was born a black girl and I grew up into a black woman. I was once a queer hippie kid searching for peace in a New England boarding school because home could no longer hold me. I was once a masculine-identified lesbian, a femme-loving stud who was afraid to love other masculine folk—I was never told it was okay for us to love one another and that our love was valuable too. And today I write this as a black transman, queer boi, lover of love. I chose this life.

But what do we do with the scars? I have scars. Visible scars from falling as a kid. Visible scars from nights of self-inflicted cutting in high school. Visible scars from my recent double mastectomy. Those scars are easier for me to deal with because I know where to find them. I know what might irritate the recent scars on my chest. But what of the scars that you can't see?

You ever go so deep and remember the things you didn't know you were reminding yourself to forget?

Sadness. It haunts me. It sits on me sometimes and I wish I could move it, transition it.

I only recently learned that the sadness I carry is not just my own. It was inherited. Both my mother and father struggle with depression, but no one ever told me. I thought I was alone, and we still struggle to talk about it—how things from way back when still hurt us. And how we never got to take a break after losing so much.

Once I asked my mother about crack. I asked her about my dad. I asked her how she loved him. I asked her why she made me love him even though he hurt us over and over.

She told me she felt shame. She told me that I was the only one she could talk to because everyone thought she was crazy to stay, but she loved him. That he was her husband and my father, and she knew his heart. Crack changed him. Crack destroyed so many black love stories.

She told me that it was only in the last couple of years that she had stopped sleeping with her purse under her pillow for fear of having it stolen. She hasn't been with my my dad in more than six years. Scars…

If you cared about it, you had better lock it up in the back room. I remember the frustration of forgetting, forgetting that nothing was safe unless you locked it away. I remember when something of my big brother's got stolen. I remember how angry he was. I remember how guilty I felt because it was my father who was the addict, not my big brother's father.

I remember God. God and my mother were the only people I was allowed to talk to. We kept secrets from the outside world—we built our own. But we needed more. We couldn't save my dad. I couldn't save my mother. I learned the most radical thing I could do was figure out how to save myself. We all have to save ourselves. We all have to find our way toward healing and forgiveness. And it is a long road.

I am a black transman who loves men and women. I am a man who is just now learning to love my femininity. I was a girl named Kiana once. She survived a summer of sexual abuse when she was eight. When she told the truth there was no counseling. There was no processing, only a *fast girl* who needed to be watched closely. I prayed to God for forgiveness. Guilt hurt, and I started getting migraines. I moved with guilt in my heart, guilt as my center. I didn't want to be bad, but I felt bad. I carried guilt when I left my mother with my father, but it was the only way I could get free. I had to leave.

I am Kai. I had to leave. I had to move into this new body.

Sometimes we don't get what we deserve because we don't know our own value.

WE deserve great love, laughter, poetry, sweetness, sunshine, and smiles.

WE deserve true love, open and honest.

We deserve healthy love—love, a home where you don't have to hide what is most valuable in order to keep it.

I write with love for you, brothers, the agape kind.

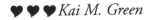*Kai M. Green*

***

DEAR KAI, KIESE, DARNELL, AND MYCHAL,

Damn, you guys are bringing up some things that are making me go deep within. Just two months ago, I was finally able to voluntarily move out of my parents' house. FYI: I said voluntarily because I spent a decade in what some of my brothers call Mr. Gilmore's house, aka the big house. I've been in prison for the last ten years of my life.

I'm black and from Brooklyn, so my spending time in Mr. Gilmore's house ain't no thing nowadays. Y'all know the stats about black men in prison, so I will spare the choir the gospel. But, man that ain't the half of it all. I got people telling me that I need to see a quack because they think I'm emotionless...gotta admit, I think I am too. I mean, I care about a whole lot of people and things and issues. In fact, my whole life is dedicated to caring. That's why I do the work that I do, mentoring and nurturing the hood to be safer and so on. But, brothers, I'm numb when it comes to deep feelings. I don't quite know when it happened, but I might be messed up in the head, at least by therapist co-pay standards.

It's late and I don't feel like giving you all the whole book of my life right now, but I will give you all a little context as to how I became as emotionless as I am. This is going to be confessions on speed, so keep up.

Ready?

Last of three kids, older brother, good...no, great parents. Older brother hated the crap outta me (no clue why...well, I have some ideas), nerdy kid, jumped badly at fourteen, almost raped at gunpoint at fourteen by some random bitchassmofo (had my first nut at the same time), lost my virginity at eighteen, shot at eighteen (doctor said I'd never walk the same again...proved him wrong), arrested for first-degree murder at twenty (though I never killed anyone), sentenced to a dozen plus five at twenty-two, released at thirty, doing great things for myself and others since then.

LOL, maybe I need some therapy. I don't know.

What I do know is that I meet great women who want to love me, who I want to love back, at least in my mind, but I have a hard time replicating that want in my heart. So, y'all are talking about loving, and I'm talking about loving. I love myself and others to the bitter end, and I'm proud of myself for surviving so much unscathed. I'm the easiest person to get along with, or disagree with.

I write well. That's what folks tell me. I speak well. That's what folks tell me. I inspire others. That's what folks tell me. Don't get me wrong, I believe all of that stuff, and I thank God for it (I was raised as a Jehovah's Witness, BTW, though I'm not really an active JW right now because I drink and screw and all that good stuff, though I don't cuss on the regular), but all this surviving and experience is so f'ing much at times. You know, my pops once told me that you shouldn't suffocate the spirit, meaning you shouldn't hold in how you feel for someone.

Oh, did you expect me to give some sort of anecdotal moral to that quote, like you're taught to in English class? Like, you shouldn't leave a paragraph without finishing your point? Nah, I ain't got the answer, homies. I guess that's what I'll leave for you all to finish. You know, keep the flow going.

Bless,

Marlon Peterson

Kanye West and HaLester Myers
Are Better at Their Jobs...

MY GRANDMOTHER MARRIED A BEAUTIFUL brown troll named HaLester "Les" Myers twenty years ago. The Christmas before last, Les slumped across from me in Grandma's gaudy pink throne while she finished making supper. I watched the still water flooding the gutters of Les's sleepy eyes, the way his nappy gray chin folded snugly into the top of those musty blue overalls, and I knew that this dusty joker really believed what he had said the night before about Kanye West and the importance of treating females like cats.

"Look at Les over there faking sleep," my Aunt Sue said from the doorway. "He 'sleep? Get up, Les! Time to eat. Wake him up, Kie."

Les's sweaty face didn't move. His chest didn't heave in or out. But his fingers, which doubled as raggedy overstuffed cigars, dug deeper into both arms of Grandma's favorite chair.

HaLester Myers was preparing for takeoff.

The night before, on Christmas Eve, I joined Les outside in his runaway spot. No matter the time of day or night, Les was likely to clutch his yellow folding chair and lumber out to the right side of Grandma's porch. Really, unless he was drunk, Les's runaway spot was the only place my Grandma allowed him to do the 2.5 things he'd mastered in his 83 years on earth: 1) sipping that Crown Royal Black, and 2.5) balancing a dangling Newport on his bottom lip while telling the loudest lies you've ever heard in your life.

I'm convinced Les tells so many loud lies not necessarily because he's deceptive, but because he has no inside voice and Grandma rarely lets him talk over volume five inside her house. When Les is lying about being a forty-ninth degree Mason, his voice sounds like flat tires rolling over jagged gravel. When he's lying about what he did to the dog, cat, or car of the white man who "ain't know how to pay a nigga right," his voice sounds like burning bubble wrap. No matter what Les is lying about, all of his lies have an acidic slow drip to them, and nearly all the lies carry stories rooted in what "the black man" deserves.

This Christmas Eve, like every Christmas Eve in Forest, Mississippi, I grabbed a chair from the kitchen before we lit our fireworks and walked out to where I knew Les would be sipping that Black.

"Les, you know who Kanye West is, right?" I asked him and sat down under some droopy white Christmas lights.

"Kanye!" he said. "Say do I know Kanye?" Les stood up like he did whenever he told lies in his runaway spot. When he stood up and you stayed seated, Les could look down at you and say one of his favorite lying sentences—"Look up here, man"—with more precision.

"Look up here, man," he said and lit another Newport. "I been know'n Kanye. His mama come over to the Public Museum when I was working security in Milwaukee around 1986, I believe it was. I been told her little Kanye was go'n be a prophet. On one hand," Les slung out his right hand, "you got Kanye telling the white man the truth about what the black man deserve, see?"

He put down the Black and slung out his other hand.

"On the other hand, look up here, you got Obama deciding who deserve to get what in America. White man can't stand that. Obama and Kanye, they the same, though, son. Yes they is."

I was confused. "Wait," I told him. "So Obama is deciding what white folks deserve and Kanye is telling white folks what black folks deserve? And you're saying white folks hate both of them for that?"

Les tapped me on my knee and bent at his waist until he was inches away from my face. The Newport smoke, his Crown Royal Black breath, and that eighty-three-year-old tartar confused me even more. I couldn't figure out whether to breathe through my nose or my mouth.

"Fifty years ago," he said, "I'm saying that the white man woulda hung both of them niggas over yonder in that field just for thinking about doing what they did. Yes he would, too!"

It wasn't until Les asked the question, "Kanye sang them songs, don't he?" that I knew for sure that Kanye West had never sculpted a beat, never sung a hook, and never rapped a bar in the mind of HaLester Myers. Les had never heard of Taylor Swift. He didn't know Kanye's mother had passed and definitely didn't know that *My Beautiful Dark Twisted Fantasy*, Kanye's most acclaimed album, had just been released a few weeks earlier.

To Les, Kanye West was simply the young black man with the goatee and the boxed jaw, who told the world that black folks drowning in poisonous water deserved more from the president of our country.

"The white man give Kanye that microphone 'cause he ain't think there was no way he could tell the truth," Les told me and sat down. "After all them Afghanese that Bush killed, now he claim Kanye the worst thing that happened to him in eight years? White man'll say anything, you hear me?" Les said and stood up again.

"Look up here, man. Anything! He believe everything he say, too. Just like Brett Favre..."

At this point, even though it was cold for Mississippi, Les started to sweat. I knew I was supposed to ask Les another question about Brett Favre, but I'd heard the Brett Favre set of lies two Christmases in a row. I wanted the Kanye West set of lies for this Christmas.

Les put his Black back down again and pulled a rag out of the front pocket of his overalls. I watched him wipe from the middle of his George Jefferson all the way down to the base of his thick neck.

"You okay?" I asked him.

"I reckon I am," he said and picked up his bottle again. "You ain't hot, son?"

"I'm good," I told him. "Back in the day, you think the white man would hang a black woman for saying the same thing Kanye said?"

Les looked up at me and took a few more drags off that Newport. "Naw," he said in his best inside voice that was both formal and afraid. "Naw. I don't reckon he would, but you never know. I ain't one for guessing what a female gon do."

I wasn't sure how Les moved from never knowing if a black woman would have been lynched, to guessing what a "female" would do, but I just nodded and kept listening.

"You got a better chance of winning every dime they got off in them Indian casinos." He blew the smoke toward his work boots. "Expect the unexpected from a female, son. Care for them like you care for your cat. Just don't never trust na one if you can help it. If you do, that's the end of you..."

I stood up and looked down at Les. He kept his slowly blinking eyes directed at the Mexican trailer park next to Grandma's house.

I felt like smacking Les in his heart for implying that my Grandma should be treated like a cat. But mostly, I felt a healthy heaping of something else, a superbly satisfying something else that I hadn't needed to feel since the day Kanye's latest classic, *My Beautiful Dark Twisted Fantasy*, was officially released.

The day the CD drops, I'm invited to give a talk at Columbia Law School on black literary imagination for Kimberle Crenshaw's class, "Colorblindness and the Law." I had the bootleg of the CD for two weeks, but my boy, Hua, and I still dart to Best Buy in between classes to get two originals.

On my way to the train station in Poughkeepsie, I play the first minute of the actual CD in my car.

Then I replay it.

Shit is just too good.

I play the last minute of the album in the parking lot of the station. And I replay it.

Mercy.

I love that Kanye West, the self- and society-anointed international asshole, not only frames his album with the questions, "Can we get much higher?" and "Who will survive in America?" but also borders his fantasy with the faux British voice of Nicki Minaj and the grainy revolutionary voice of Gil Scott-Heron. Within this frame, with all the guest verses and distorted vocals, it's obvious Kanye West believes that plenty of voices other than his own also deserve to be explored in his beautiful dark twisted fantasy.

I step on the Metro North and folks are in their usual pre–New York states of mind. Heads nearly down. Fists almost clenched. Purses, backpacks, empty McDonald's bags, and pleather briefcases damn near snug against puffy coats, blouses, and suit jackets.

Unusually though, there are lots of downward-turned heads bobbing as familiar static came from a few headphones. Different tracks from Kanye's twisted fantasy compete for space and time on that train.

Literally.

For the sleepy-eyed woman across from me, it's "Runaway." For the man two seats behind me, it sounds like "Gorgeous." For a kid I know who got on at Beacon, it's "Power."

I get into a dollar cab at 125th and I'm shocked that the driver looks like he could be one of my students named Jacob or Seth. I'm even more shocked that JacobSeth is bumping "Blame Game."

"This Kanye shit is unreal," JacobSeth says.

"Yeah," I tell him, more weirded out that JacobSeth is driving a dollar cab than the fact that JacobSeth just assumes I love Kanye West, too. "It is kinda crazy."

By the time I get to the law school, Chris Rock is asking the voice formerly known as that of a real woman, "Who reupholstered your pussy?"

I get out of the cab, Yeezy's reupholstered pussy behind me, wondering if this is really still Harlem and thankful that I'm from little ol' Jackson, Mississippi. I make my way upstairs.

Kim's class is beyond gratifying. We break. We listen. We build. We wonder. I bounce.

On the way out, Kim asks two of her students, one a Korean-American woman and one an Iranian-American man, to hail a taxi for me. It's a loving, pragmatic gesture, she assures me, because cabs ain't got no love for black men going uptown.

Once we're out on 116th, Kim's students decide they can be more effective if each goes to either side of the street. I think about "Blame Game," "Runaway," and "So Appalled," and I ask the woman what side I should go to. I'm wondering if she thinks my talk was typical academic bullshit. I'm hoping the woman remembers the comment I made about packaged misogyny being more lucrative than rhyming about slanging dope if you're a rapper, and nearly as lucrative as uncritically using guns, gunshots, and criminal tactics to sell movie tickets if you're not.

The woman tells me to stay on her side of the street. I can't tell if she's giving me rhythm but I'm leaning toward maybe. I look across the street at the Iranian-American cat, then look down at her one more time.

"I should probably wait over there with him," I tell her.

It feels so good to walk away from this woman, believing not only that she thinks I'm slightly dope, but that she also thinks I'm unlike all those other men when it comes to spitting game.

Across 116th, the Iranian-American cat and I wait. And the taxis pass. And we wait. And I wave and smile at the Korean-American woman. I act like it doesn't all sting and feel so good at the same time.

Finally, I'm in a dollar cab headed back to 125th and ultimately back to Poughkeepsie, wondering how to explore with colorful profundity the absurd privilege and policing that exists around the delicate shadows of grown American black boys. It isn't until the next day in front of a computer screen that I realize that intentionally and unintentionally, just maybe, Kanye has done that and so much more with his beautiful dark twisted fantasy.

Instead of standing up and saying all that to Les that night, I continue looking down on him, watching his chest heave in and out. I want to tell him that if he really listened to Kanye West, he would hear that Kanye wants maligned folks to get what they deserve.

Poor black folks from New Orleans deserved more, so Kanye said, "George Bush doesn't care about black people."

Beyonce deserved more, so Kanye said, "Taylor, I'ma let you finish, but Beyonce had one of the greatest videos of all time."

Queer brothers deserved more, so Kanye said, "I been discriminating against gays...and I wanna come on TV and tell my rappers, just tell my friends, Yo, stop it, fam..."

Black kids in Chicago deserved more, so Kanye said, "Man, killing's some wack shit."

Listeners of American popular music deserved more than formulaic noise, so Kanye West offered us eight years of GOOD music. In those eight years, Kanye managed to collapse, carve, and distort disparate sounds rooted in the black musical traditions into newly shaped inescapable musical experiences. His work did more than challenge conventional composition. Whether it's *College Dropout, Late Registration, 808s and Heartbreak,* or *Watch the Throne,* Kanye's work literally dared us to revise our expectations of sound.

Precisely because Kanye is able to give us so much more than we actually deserve, I need to tell Les that Kanye West, that boxjawed American virtuoso who told the white man the truth, is eons better at his job than Les is at lying, and I am at writing, but when it comes to exploring women (you know, "females," "cats," "bitches," "hoes," "pussies," "Kelly Rowlands," "hood rats," "good girls," "sluts," "light-skinned girls," and now "Perfect Bitches"), Kanye West ain't really using his voice or his art right.

This actually makes him just like almost every other virtuoso and mediocre American man I've ever read, watched, or heard.

Kanye West is better than those jokers, though.

He has proven himself good enough, brave enough, conceptually genius enough, compassionate enough, and now rich enough to use his voice to explore, with prickly honesty and dramatic irony, what black women deserve—as well as the ways he is encouraged to obsessively dismember, soulfully mutilate, and straight dis the fuck out of women in order to move units and feel like a manlier man.

I get where it comes from. We were all fed the same thing. As inspirational as we found Dre's music, Snoop's flow, and Cube's criticism, an articulated fear and hatred of black women was part of what made them so nationally attractive. Like nearly all of our lyrical pedagogues, the MCs that came a generation before Kanye practiced a form of spectacular psychological and/or emotional dismantling of black women passed down by the practices, policies, and patriarchy of America.

Chuck D and Flav told us all that women were "blind to the facts" of who they were because they watched the wrong television shows. Slick Rick warned us to pre-emptively treat women like prostitutes since all they did was "hurt and trample." Too Short painted the freakiest of tales and constantly reminded us that the correct pronunciation of the words "woman" and/or "girl" was "bitch."

Big Daddy Kane and Nice and Smooth let us know that no matter what we heard from Too Short, pimping was never easy. The Geto Boys showed us how to kick a woman in the ass if she claimed to be pregnant with our baby. Before we elected a modern Falstaff with hoish tendencies to the White House, MC Ren taught us how to gang-rape the fourteen-year-old daughter of a preacher and sodomize any women "saying that they never would suck a dick."

So yeah, that's what we were taught, but at what point does listening to artists obsessively encourage manipulative relationships, sociopathic deception, and irresponsible sex with women doubling as accessorized pussy become not just destructive, but really, really boring? If Kanye West won't, or maybe even can't, explore the meat of that question, isn't he still too great to exploit it?

That's some of what I wanted to tell Les after he said that thing about treating females like cats. Instead of saying any of it, though,

I just hovered over him in his runaway spot, feeling extra good about myself for wanting to say any of it at all.

A month or so later, I sat in front of a computer screen in New York and wrote a piece critiquing both Les for reducing my grandma to a cat and Kanye for the destructive gender politics in his art. I ended the piece with what I thought was a harpoon to Les's gizzard: "I should have asked Les if he deserved to ever have his hand held by a woman."

The essay generally, and that sentence specifically, helped me run away from the truth, from reckoning, from meaningful change.

I don't want to run any more.

I am better at fucking up the lives of a few women who have unconditionally loved me than Les is at lying and Kanye West is at making brilliant American music. And even worse than the bruising parts of Kanye's art, the paranoid femiphobia of HaLester Myers, the pimpish persona of Stevie J, the abusive gender politics of Paul Ryan and Todd Akin, and the thousands of confused brothers out there who think "misogyny" is the newest Italian dish at Olive Garden, I have intimately fucked up women's lives while congratulating myself for not being Kanye West, HaLester Myers, Stevie J, Paul Ryan, Todd Akin, or the brothers who like that misogyny with a few breadsticks.

Even before this essay, I wanted the fact that I've read, and taken notes on, everything ever published by Audre Lorde, bell hooks, Imani Perry, dream hampton, and Rebecca Walker to prove to everyone—especially women I'm interested in—that I'm way too thoughtful to be a dickhead. I wanted folks to know that I've made my male students reckon with being born potential rapists, and that I've defended black girls in need of abortions from rabid pro-lifers at abortion clinics in Mississippi. I wanted women to know that I was a man who would always ask, "Are you okay? Are you sure you want to do this?"

I couldn't wait to tell some men—but only when in the presence of women—how sexism, like racism and that annoying American inclination to cling to innocence, was as present in our blood as oxygen. When asked to prove it, I'd dutifully spit some sorry-sounding mash-up of Michael Eric Dyson, Cornel West, and Mark Anthony Neal. But just like them, I never said that I know I'm sexist, misogynist, and typical because I have fucked up the lives of some women in ways that they would never fuck up my life. I never said that I've used black feminism as a convenient shield, as a wonderful sleep aid, and as a rusted shank to damage others who would do everything to avoid damaging me.

Of course, it's more complicated than that. And of course there are all kinds of qualifications and conditions I want to explore. But beneath all of that conditional bullshit is a lot of ugly.

This is what I refused to admit, not only when I looked down at Les for making his comment about females and cats that night, but also the following day, Christmas Day, when Les sat across the room from me in Grandma's pink throne and wouldn't wake up.

Grandma looked up at me with a fear I'd never seen in her eyes as I rubbed melting ice cubes on Les's temple and his bottom lip.

As Les was laid out on a stretcher and lifted into the back of an ambulance, his eyes still didn't open, but huge tears dripped slowly into his ears. With his eyes still closed, Les cried that cry that comes from way deeper than hurt.

He cried all the way to the hospital.

After we were at the hospital a while, the doctors said Les's blood alcohol level was almost .35. He had nearly drank himself to death. When Grandma went in the room with him, she told Les that she had a strap in her purse and she was going to whup his ass if he ever scared her like that again.

When Grandma left the room, I hugged her as tight as I could. She kept saying into my chest, "I don't know why, Kie. I just don't even know." Then I went in and gripped Les's thick fingers. He mumbled something about a "seven" and clutched the front of his overalls, which were now drooping around his belly button.

"You gotta pee?" I asked him.

"Three-fif sheh-bilm," he said.

"357?"

I reached for the front of Les's overalls and slowly opened the pocket. "Hide it from the white man," he slurred.

I pulled out a loaded .357.

I put the gun in my coat pocket. Even after all he'd said the night before and all he'd done this night, it fucked me up that Les was still worried about the white man.

"Les, gotdamn, man," I said to him. "You gotta do better than this."

"I know," he mumbled in the smallest, most terrifying voice I'd ever heard him use. "I know." Then he pulled me closer and whispered in my ear, "I'm shorry, man, for what I shed."

I pulled away from Les and just looked at him. He wasn't in his right mind, but even in his wrong mind I wondered if he knew that what he said the day before about females being like cats was wrong. Maybe he actually knew that part of me wanted to bust his head to the whitest of white meat for indirectly talking mess about Grandma. Or maybe he really knew that most of me was an opportunistic coward always in search of instant deliverance.

The next night, my grandma—the tiny, complicated, hardheaded woman responsible for whatever integrity and freedom I have—fell into a diabetic coma. The same white EMTs came to the house, took her to the hospital, and placed her one room down from where Les was the night before.

When Grandma finally regained consciousness, I lied to Les and told him that she wanted to see him. I sat in the chair next to Grandma while Les, in those same blue overalls, came in and held one of Grandma's hands in between both of his.

"Doctor say you ain't doing what you supposed to do," he told her.

"I did what I was supposed to do," Grandma said with a weak voice and slow twitching eyes. "Mary and them had something to say about everything I ate, so I end up not eating enough."

"Okay, okay. Just telling you what the doctor said to me," Les told her. "That ain't my voice. That's the doctor."

HaLester Myers wasn't lying.

And with that, Les stood there in those same stanky blue overalls, shamefully looking down into the eyes of my grandma—a supposed cat, an untrustworthy female, a blamed bitch, a few babies' mama, a ho who should run away. Les stood, not saying a word, knowing right there that my grandma deserved every bit of whatever care he had left in him. I sat there, too, looking at Les, trying hard to shake my head in slow motion.

It wouldn't move.

If I had any guts, I would have asked Les if he was holding the hand of Catherine Coleman, a human being he loved, a human being who loved him better than anyone on earth. If I were less of a man, I would have asked Les if Kanye West, he, or I deserved to ever have our hands held by a woman.

If I would have asked, HaLester Myers would not have told a lie.

Reasonable Doubt and the Lost Presidential Debate of 2012

October 29, 2008, 2:15 a.m.

"I'm not wearing anything with Barack Obama's name on it," my mother tells me over the phone.

I'm at work in upstate New York. Mama is at home in Central Mississippi.

"I'm serious," she says. "I'm not trying to have some redneck knock me upside my head, or run my car off in the Pearl River over a damn Obama bumper sticker." Mama wants me to say something. "And you shouldn't either, Kie."

I make myself laugh until my throat burns, but Mama doesn't even chuckle.

"I know you," she says. "And I know you'll do whatever I tell you not to do, but a hardhead makes a soft behind when you're dealing with entitled folks who never learned how to lose."

My mother is being my mother.

As long as I can remember, Mama has slept with a .22 under her pillow, closed her blinds at 6:00 p.m., and refused to answer the door unless she has invited you a day in advance.

But that's just a millimeter of my mama's story.

One expects to hear this kind of stilted racial paranoia over Obama shirts and bumper stickers from a typical American voter, not a woman who has been a political analyst and a professor of political science for almost thirty years.

On Election Day, November 4, 2008, Mama will be on some local station in Jackson, Mississippi, prognosticating her ass off. Mama won't lie to Mississippians watching her on election night, but she damn sure won't tell them the truth either.

Whether talking about *Brown v. Board*, the Montgomery bus boycott, Meredith enrolling in Ole Miss in 1962, Freedom Summer, the Mississippi Freedom Democratic Party's bum-rush in 1964, the Civil Rights Act in the same year, the Voting Rights Act of 1965, the Swann decision in 1971, or the Civil Rights Restoration Act of 1988, Mama taught me that black Americans have always borne the brunt of domestic economic terrorism after supposed policy and political wins.

As Mama talks to me on the speaker phone about how resentment and backlash will find a way to shrink opportunities to escape poverty for black and brown Americans during an Obama presidency, I'm mm-hmm-ing her to death and looking for a T-shirt in my closet.

Hanging next to the fifteen-year-old brown polyester suit she bought for my high school graduation and a sky-blue Jackson State hoodie is the sickest Obama T-shirt you've ever seen in your life. It's black pre-washed cotton with a huge red, black, and green picture of Obama's face on it. Obama's face is liquid aluminum, like a contemplative red, black, and green Terminator 4. On the bottom, in that played-out Times New Roman, are the words, "Yes We Can."

Mama doesn't know about my RBG T4 Obama shirt.

Anyway, I wear the shirt three times a week and I'll definitely rock it tomorrow morning when I vote. Tonight, I'm imagining wearing the shirt while driving home to Mississippi for Christmas:

RBG T4 Obama shirt and I are hauling ass through Penn-sylvania, Virginia, West Virginia, Tennessee, and Alabama, in late December, our backseat covered with fifteen folded RBG T4 Obama shirts I plan on giving away to my family and friends in Jackson. I'm bumping this Mahalia Jackson/ Andre 3000 duet as I pull up to a dusty Amoco in Northern Alabama. I open the door of my truck as fourteen working-class white locals look at me and my Obama shirt with hate in their mind, envy in their hearts, and "Niggers these days" on the tips of their thin wet lips.

Within seconds, the locals are wearing my Obama shirts, sipping on Faygos, and talking that good shit with some other black Alabamans and me about the underrated importance of moral imagination and local activism in carving the policies that will mitigate the economic and social problems of our region in 2008. We're also coming up with a list of real ques-tions we want to ask at the next presidential election in 2012.

I hardly sleep, but love to dream.

When I was younger, Mama said that lack of moral imagina-tion on the part of most white folks was exactly why black girls and boys needed to be twice as good to get half as much of white Americans in our country. She said you have to pity an entitled group of people who believe black and brown folks are getting more than they deserve when they themselves have twenty times more wealth, better access to good health care, are far less likely either to go to prison or to grow up in poverty, and are five times more likely to go to college. "Don't ever let them beat you," Mama and Grandma repeated with their daily, "I love you."

Both neglected to tell me there was also a bruising, terrible price to pay for being better than intellectual white folks drunk off of American white liberal entitlement.

I learned that on my own, way up at good ol' liberal Vassar College.

"Mama," I say over the phone. "I gotta go, but I hear you."

I hang in the grainy silence, hoping that Mama will change the subject to Serena Williams or my insomnia or her recent surgery. I'm hoping Mama will tell me that God won't give us anything we can't handle or some other bloated cliché.

Instead, Mama eventually sighs and says again, "Kie, people who never learned to lose will do anything to see us not win. When they lose to Obama, they'll figure out a way to win anyway. It's just too much."

"You way too cynical, Mama," I tell her. "We got this."

"I love you, Kie," she says. "Stay safe, and pray for Michelle, Barack, and those kids."

"Mama, I thought you were saying that we should pray for us."

"It's just too much," Mama says. "This has nothing to do with politics, or public policy. Goodnight, Kie."

Mama hangs up the phone and I pull the RBG T4 T-shirt out of my closest and put it next to my red Pumas, an army-green sweatshirt, and some baggy black shorts I'll wear early tomorrow morning when I go to vote.

I'm playing it off, imagining the celebrations that will follow the election of our first black President. But not even deep down, though, I know Mama is right.

We know Mama is right.

Obama will win. *We* will win. Then we will continue to lose. And the right questions will never be honestly asked or answered. And it's all just too much.

***

November 5, 2008, 2:15 a.m.

Earlier tonight, I wore my RBG T4 Obama shirt as Barack Obama beat John McCain into a pile of All-American dust. Hundreds of Vassar College students celebrated in front of my apartment on campus. Some kids streaked, while others unknowingly remixed a traditional lynch scene by hoisting a life-size cardboard Barack Obama into the moonlit sky. Joyful sounds echoed for hours as young Americans who would never call themselves hipsters, rich, or racist morphed into patriots with chants of "USA! USA!"

One of my wonderful first-year white students walked up to me in the midst of the celebration and said, "Congratulations," like he knew I had just hit the Mega Millions or paid off my student loans.

I had done neither.

"Oh," I said. "Congratulations to you, too."

Really, I just registered it as one of those slick things "good" white folks do when confronted with splendid black American achievement. Honestly, I didn't know what the victory, the celebration in that space, or the congratulations given to us black Americans meant. I didn't know if we were celebrating Obama's victory, McCain's defeat, the end of Bush's regime, our deliverance, the possibility of a post-racist America, triumph for African-Americans, or a little bit of all those things.

When the dry, pulpy feeling got to be too much to bear, I got in my car to drive downtown, where most of the black and brown folks in Poughkeepsie live, and where a good number of folks live way below the poverty line.

The mile and a half drive from the corner of Main and Raymond to the waterfront was as quiet a drive as I'd ever experienced. No human beings were outside. There were no signs or sounds of shared celebrations.

There was no echo.

Inside those apartments, houses, and buildings, I assumed folks were smiling from the inside out. I also assumed most of those folks were wondering how retribution for this splendid black

American achievement would be played out on their bodies, pockets, spirits, and minds. I wondered if the right questions could ever really change anything, and the right questions seemed further and further away.

***

October 29, 2012, 2:15 a.m.

I'd like to thank President Obama and Governor Romney for giving us twenty minutes in this last/lost debate of 2012. Thanks to both of you for agreeing to release this transcript after November 6. If I ask a question you don't want to answer, you can say, "That's that shit I don't like," courtesy of Chief Keef, and I will do my best to move on to another question. You have two "That's that shit I don't likes" at your disposal. Instead of a coin toss, whoever best answers our first question will have the option of going first or second.

Our first question comes from a young woman in Brooklyn: "How would you describe the color of Donald Trump's face?"

> **ROMNEY:** I'd have to say he's just tan. Maybe I'm missing something but I'd call it a supple kind of pink.

> **OBAMA:** Listen, I've gotta go with the color of watered-down Tang.

Damn. That's good, man. Really good. Would you like to go first or second, President Obama?

> **OBAMA:** First.

President Obama, you signed the Fair Sentencing Act, a historic piece of legislation that narrows the crack and powder cocaine sentencing disparity from 100:1 to 18:1, and for the first time eliminates the mandatory minimum sentence for simple possession of crack cocaine. While this was long overdue, wouldn't a real Fair Sentencing Act also ensure that elite American colleges, universities, and gated communities are policed for drug use, drug abuse, and drug distribution as much as urban areas currently are policed—especially since most incarcerated Americans are poor black and brown nonviolent drug offenders?

OBAMA: While I agree that we need to think about how we police particular groups of Americans more than others, I'm not sure it's the role of the president to tinker with policing practices, especially ones that substantially impact the prison-industrial complex. We wanted to make the sentencing guidelines fair and we did.

Is 18:1 fair?

OBAMA: It's fairer than it was.

True, but is it fair that not one drug user, abuser, or seller at the college where I teach has gone to prison in the ten years I've been there, yet I personally know at least twenty brothers in Poughkeepsie from the same neighborhood who have been incarcerated in that same time?

ROMNEY: I don't understand the question. Those black and brown nonviolent drug offenders would have a better chance at the American dream if there were fathers in their houses. If I am elected president, I plan on creating civic organizations that go door to door in urban neighborhoods with binders of eligible, hard-working, clean black and Latino men. Prison reform and fair sentencing starts with the family, and the new American family starts with reforming fathers and families, not the government.

Daddy binders, bruh?

OBAMA: Governor Romney loves him some binders, doesn't he?

You ain't lying about that. President Obama, we incarcerate more people than any other country in the world. Why?

OBAMA: See, that's that shit I don't like. How can I answer that question? While we need to look at our incarceration practices, we also need to look at the communities we are trying to protect when we incarcerate these brothers and sisters. We've got to think of the victims, too.

President Obama: You are a black man. There are more black men in prison than any other group in the nation, and black women are the fastest-growing group of incarcerated folks in the United States. Why?

OBAMA: I think I've answered the question. I told you that was that shit I don't like.

Word? Okay then.

OBAMA: Does that count as my second "That's that shit I don't like?"

It does not. Governor Romney, how is it that the Republican Party, the self-proclaimed party of personal responsibility, never, ever, ever, ever takes any responsibility for the state of the nation or of the world?

ROMNEY: I don't understand the question.

Are you and your party responsible for any of the problems in the United States?

ROMNEY: I don't understand the question. That's that shit I don't like.

This is a two-part question from a woman in Forest, Mississippi. Governor Romney, "How can the people with the most stuff in the nation complain so much about other people who have so little wanting more stuff?"

ROMNEY: That's that shit I don't like.

Cool. That's your last "That's that shit I don't like." Governor Romney, would President Obama, the first standing president to have his citizenship questioned, have been granted the same generosity afforded George W. Bush if his failure led to the deaths of more than 3,000 Americans?

ROMNEY: I think I've answered this question. The president has the responsibility to call terrorism what it is and to do everything in his power to stop it before it starts.

OBAMA: Listen, no sitting president wants to be in the position where President Bush found himself on the morning of 9/11. Americans are by and large a forgiving people and I have done everything in my power to keep this exceptional country, the best country on the face of the earth, safe from terrorism. I take responsibilities for mistakes made along the way, but our record is strong in the area of defense, especially compared to my predecessor.

President Obama, you've talked extensively in previous debates about the incredible work of the soldiers who have lost their lives fighting for the freedom of others around the globe. It's obvious that this tragedy hurts you. Does it also hurt when you received reports of drones murdering civilians around the world?

OBAMA: Yes, it does.

ROMNEY: This is exactly the kind of apologizing the president of the United States does not need to be doing.

OBAMA: The question was does it hurt, not was I apologizing.

President Obama, would you like to apologize to the families of the civilians our drones have murdered?

OBAMA: We have tried to be as responsible as possible. Have we made some mistakes? Yes. But as commander-in-chief, I take responsibility for all those mistakes.

Would you like to apologize?

OBAMA: That's too simplistic. A lot of you work in the world of words. I respect that, but I also have to deal in the reality of action. Would you rather Americans flew those warplanes and shot down bad guys?

I think we'd rather our country not kill any more folks who have nothing to do with your beef? Can you commit to doing everything in your power to halt these drone attacks?

>**OBAMA:** My beefs? (under his breath) You a funny-ass nigga. That's that shit I don't like.

Governor Romney, I can't even spell "cosmopolitan" without spell-check and I just got a passport yesterday, so please help me out. How does the only country in the world that has actually used nuclear weapons to kill tens of thousands of people have the moral authority to tell other countries not to develop nuclear weapons?

>**ROMNEY:** Yes.

Yes, what?

>**ROMNEY:** Yes. We are the greatest country in the world and we must do everything in our power to free people from dictators?

>**OBAMA:** I can say it makes sense that the current president of the United States keeps nuclear weaponry out of the hands of reckless leaders.

Wait. What question are y'all answering? Listen for a second. By the time this election is over, you both will have spent more than $6 billion on your elections. The talking heads on Fox, CNN, and MSNBC will have been paid millions and millions of dollars to root for Team Elephant or Team Donkey, while millions of Americans are poor, homeless, and hungry. Is this ethical economic behavior from the supposed best country on the face of the earth?

>**ROMNEY:** Yes.

>**OBAMA:** Yes.

Thank you both for your time. Y'all stay lying, though. For real! How come y'all are never self-critical? Like, never. It's us, right? The voters, I mean. President Obama, I don't know how you carry all this shit on your back. I'm so sincere.

Most brothers I know can't keep a checkbook and here you are running a country.

Seriously, I can't wait to see all the things you do for our people and the world when you're out of office in 2016. A lot of folks are convinced you never had the black community's best interest at heart. I ain't gonna lie. I don't think I believe that. Is that true?

> **OBAMA:** It's not true at all. I honestly don't know how a left-leaning president makes things significantly better for black, brown, and poor Americans. It's so hard. I don't know how to do it.

We need half of that defense budget to go toward shit that makes black folks healthier. We need every classroom in predominantly black and brown cities and towns to have no more than a 12:1 student/teacher ratio. We need the best mental health services in the world for our communities. We need to stop throwing brothers and sisters in jail for drugs. We need you to be honest, more than anything. Just be honest, man. I know you know all of this. You just confuse me, man.

If those heartbroken fucks out there don't find a way to hurt you and your family, you're going to do so much when you're free. You ever wonder if you'll ever be free, though? I mean, thank you for putting the country on your back and taking up the national slack, but the truth is that our unethical, morally suspect nation doesn't deserve an ethical or moral president. That's that shit no one admits.

Anyway, thank you for being a slightly better president than the nation deserves, even if you're unable to be the president that black and brown folks here really need. Think about what would happen if you just quit before your term was up in 2016 because you realized there was no way to be a just and honest American president. I know your heart hurts, man. But maybe you could use your time more effectively if you weren't president. Think about what I'm saying, okay?

> **ROMNEY:** What about me? I'd like equal time.

You? You were born rich. You will die rich. Help the country by teaching your people how to be just and thoughtful losers. I'm so sincere. Sadly, it's one of our only hopes. Sharing means that perpetual winners have to be okay losing sometimes. You're encouraging murder and you don't even care.

> **ROMNEY:** I want to apologize for going over my allotment, but with all due respect, that's that shit I don't like.

Lord have mercy!

Eulogy for Three Black Boys Who Lived

I.

Mama wanted me to love Michael Jackson the way she did, but I couldn't because all I could see was his work. My mama, a fifty-eight-year-old woman from Forest, Mississippi, grew up looking horizontally at Michael Jackson and his brothers. Mama heard not only the Jackson 5's work, but also their asphalted African-American journey to artistic, economic, and emotional freedom. As a black girl who moved every summer from Mississippi to Milwaukee with her singing sisters, my mother's life played country cousin to the contoured place from which the Jackson's bended notes sprang. Mama moved through the world a virtuosic, curious, confused, defiantly capable black girl in the schizophrenic post–*Brown v. Board* United States. Like Michael, Mama was the child of two beautiful, always persistent, and often destructive parents.

Let Mama tell it, she grew up different, alone, the "peculiar dove" in a caring but limited nest. Let her sisters Sue and Linda tell it, each of them was the peculiar dove longing for belonging. My aunts and Mama tell the story of my grandmother working hard to get them their first stereo and first record during the Christmas of 1969. The record was a 45 with "I Want You Back" on the A-side and "Who's Loving You" on the B-side. After huddling in the living room and listening to both sides of the 45 over and over, Mama remembers telling Grandma thank you, then wading through chinaberry bushes and climbing a hanging moss tree where she wrote about Michael Jackson's happy-sad voice, her hatred for nasty Isaiah Horde, and the colorful isolation she felt from the world.

As a single working parent in the late 70s, Mama worked to create music despite the heartbreaking noise of flimsy job security, mangled romantic relationships, and unpaid utility bills. Mama found some order through transference and restriction. I could watch our twelve-inch black-and-white television for one hour a day. I could go outside only after I wrote an essay using words from the dictionary that neither of us knew. I couldn't eat much sugar or salt, or guzzle that cold drank, unless Mama was there to okay it. Playing any form of hip-hop was always a beatable offense, while all music played on my single tape-deck radio could never exceed six on the volume...except for Michael Jackson.

When Mama and I weren't jamming until all hours of the night to the *Off the Wall* tape I got for Christmas, I was in my room listening to the tape alone. There I could sing the songs the way I wanted. I could be as weird and fascinated as I wanted to be by its minimalist cover art. The *Off the Wall* cover foreshadowed part of my relationship with Michael Jackson. Like a lot of folks, I'd be mesmerized by the movement of Michael's feet while wondering a lot about his face.

The contrast between the dense black of Michael's high-watered tuxedo slacks and the glow of his white socks up against a haggard brick wall created a depth, or at least a crease, into which I could easily slip. Deep in that crease, it's easy to say that I wanted to be Michael Jackson. But I don't think that's really true. Didn't we all want to work, work it like, and be worked by Michael Jackson? We wanted to dress like Michael dressed, sing like Michael sang, and move through the world the way Michael moved, all while he was working for us. And we tried hard, too, didn't we, over and over again in mirrors, at dances, in bedrooms, on stages, in classrooms, at parties, in our dreams?

Michael's work post *Thriller* changed the way we consumed music. Lots of black artists I deeply respect have said that Michael was ours on *Off the Wall* and then became the property of the world post *Thriller*. I've said that shit too, but I'm not so sure about that anymore. And it's not only because Mama and her generation had a much more mature love of Michael Jackson than we did. It's just that I am sure that while Michael belonged to music pre *Thriller*, and post *Thriller*, the music video—as a form, and as a workable televisual entity—belonged to him. In forcing MTV to play black music videos, Michael's work dictated to us the evocative narratives in the songs we loved. Where all of us had made up a thousand scenes, characters, and various familiar details of our lives to songs like "Rock With You" or "She's Out of My Life," we now knew Michael's version of the narrative that went along with "Billie Jean," "Beat It," "Thriller," "Say Say Say," and "Smooth Criminal." As much as possible, Michael's narrative imagination became ours. Hence the story of where you were, what you were doing, what you felt when you first saw "Thriller" or "Beat It" is as vivid for us as the videos we imagined while listening to *Off the Wall*.

On August 29, 2013, Michael Jackson, the greatest American worker of my life, would have been fifty-five years old. Michael's work connected us. His work made us wear pants that flooded and strange white sequined gloves borrowed from our grandma's usher uniform. His work encouraged us save up lunch money, birthday money, Christmas money, and *found* money for the *Beat It* jacket with the zippers that didn't work. His work bullied us into celebrating the presence of a confessional, a plea, and an incredible physical ferocity in one audiovisual setting. His work nudged us into accepting a cardboard kind of androgyny, though we didn't know what that meant. His work redefined rhythm, rhythmic abrasion, and colorful darkness while moaning "look at me" and "look at you" and "it hurts if you look at me too hard." Michael's work was our Badman, our trickster, our tragic mulatto, our Pinocchio, our boyfriend, our girlfriend, all at once.

Most of us all remember where we ran, or where we wanted to run, after we watched Michael turn around with those dirty yolk-yellow eyes, grinning like he'd escaped the whupping of a lifetime, at the end of the "Thriller" video. We don't just remember his many moonwalks; we remember "Motown 25," the way his work brought us out of our seats and made us wonder if we were watching some Spielberg special effect. We worried and dropped our cool when we heard Michael had burned his curl while shooting that Pepsi commercial, but even then we never ever thought he could die, not before us.

As we've grown into our late twenties, thirties, and forties, we've become more capable of looking and listening horizontally at Michael Jackson, the way our parents always have. In a nasty twist of fate, we've been forced to reckon with our greatest American worker being a paroled American black boy genius from Gary, Indiana, who performed in white face while begging us to "shum on." Michael Jackson, like us, didn't really know what to do with the eyes of white folks. He seemed to believe that one could find asylum from the aesthetic burdens of blackness in the creation of ultra-black music and a parodying of white skin and features. We wanted to tell him, "We get it, but you ain't gotta hide no more. Not you! Magic can just be magic."

And in our own way, we told him exactly that. And we did reckon. We knew, and know intimately, that there are more ways to perform in white face than to bleach your skin, slice off your nose, and fry your hair. Fifty years ago, James Baldwin wrote that it is only in "his" music that the American Negro is able to tell "his" story. Baldwin, as boldly imaginative as he was (even though he wrote about Michael in a paragraph for a piece called "Freaks and Ideal of American Manhood"), could not forecast what Michael Jackson's work would do to the way we heard and saw our American character in our American stories. Michael worked to entertain us and, at the end, like most dutiful workers, he seemed to believe that even if your boss is a deceptive vulture, the customer is always right.

Like a lot of you, I'll spend what would have been Michael's fifty-fifth birthday waddling in the regrettable American mess Michael Jackson left and wondering if we failed to let him know how thankful we were for his work. I cry not when I think about his dead whitened body, his growing children, or the really predictable way his family has carried on in his death. I cry when I see my grandma watching Aunt Sue, Aunt Linda, and Mama huddled around the new record player in their tiny living room in Forest, Mississippi. It's 1969, and Grandma is behind the door swelling with pride as all three of her children listen to that last note of "Who's Loving You" spin safely away into a series of grainy hiccups. Neither Grandma, Aunt Linda, Aunt Sue, or Mama can imagine a day forty-four years in the future when their grandson, nephew, and son will tell whoever is listening that *the greatest American worker of our time, a curious little paroled black boy from Gary who felt compelled to work in white face while changing the way music sounds and looks, would have been fifty-five today, but he is dead.*

Michael, you were so fucked up, and so are we. We see you, really. And we love what we see. We know you were tired, and now maybe you can take care of yourself. Please don't worry, though. Your work ain't going nowhere. Get your rest, brother. Your work is here.

II.

Not so deep down, we all know that safety is an illusion, that only character melds us together. That's why most of us do everything we can (healthy and unhealthy) to ward off that real feeling of standing alone so close to the edge of the world. Bernard Jeffrey McCullough was happy to be there with us.

Bernie Mac knew that vulnerability was our kryptonite and kryptonite our only chance at a compassionate life. He became a comedian at five years old. In 1963, Mac walked into a room where his mother was weeping and asked her why she was crying. Minutes later, Bill Cosby was introduced on *The Ed Sullivan Show*. As his mother's tears turned into laughs, Mac promised his mother that night that he would become a comedian.

Long before Bernie Mac's network show, he had the ability to look like he was never supposed to be on stage. He was the most wonderfully regular, perpetually forty-three-year-old looking black man you have ever seen in your life. Mac looked forty-three at thirty-two, forty-three at forty-three, and forty-three at fifty. And something about that eased our suffering and reconnected us, to home, to our uncles. He didn't seem desperate to be funnier, sexier, skinnier, tougher, richer, whiter, or blacker. Whether we watched him on stage, television, or the big screen, a huge part of us always believed that he was too wonderfully black and home for mainstream appeal. The racially myopic parts of us couldn't understand how white folks, Asian Americans, and Latinos could feel Bernie Mac. It wasn't at all that we thought Mac and home were too small to shine in that arena. Mac, who really was the best of home, simply seemed too textured, sincere, ironic, and, really, too much like our uncle to be fully accepted and celebrated by anyone but us.

A significant amount of the work of all performers is done before they open their mouths. In Mac's roaming eyes, his long elegance, his toothy scowl that looked like a smile and his toothy smile that looked like a scowl, we felt the one uncle at the family reunion who fabricates the best stories, mixed with the sole uncle who refuses to eyeball-fuck the sexy young "second" niece that all the other uncles are trying to convince themselves isn't really related by blood. Long before he opened his mouth on stage, television, or the big screen, that was Bernie Mac to us.

Mac lacked the all-out freakish comic ability of Eddie Murphy and the agitating political savvy of Chappelle. He came into our world via Def Comedy Jam, not as the heir apparent like Martin Lawrence, Joe Torry, or Jamie Foxx. Like Pryor, and the lesser-known Robin Harris, Bernie Mac seemed happy to share the experience of suffering on the edge of the world with us.

For younger black boys in the late 80s, Robin Harris was familiar enough to be that super uncle we all had. He was black, irreverent, big-eyed, stout, caring, reckless, and, most important to his comedy, he had that just happy-to-be-alive glow. Like Mac, Harris probably came out of his mother's womb looking twenty-five years old. By thirty, he looked forty-five. And by thirty-six, Robin Harris was dead.

Like Mac, Harris's most famous bit involved caring for bad-ass kids. In Harris's bit, he takes his girlfriend and her son, along with his girlfriend's friend, BeBe, and her four bad-ass kids to Disneyland. Of course, BeBe's kids have never been anywhere, so they tear Disneyland to pieces. BeBe's kids jump Mickey Mouse, cut off Donald Duck's feet, and chase Blood and Crips alike out of the park. And on the "It's a Small World" ride, Harris would say that the children, led by the three-year-old who "can talk and shit in his Pampers at the same time," jump out of the boat and start grabbing their dicks and strutting through the water, growling, "Smawl Wuhl! Smawl Wuhl! We...BeBe's kids. We don't die. We...multiply."

Bernie Mac also wanted to explore familial desperation and loss of innocence, not in the hope of reinforcing safety or taking anyone away from the edge, but in order to bring himself to the edge with us. Mac's fifteen-minute performance in *The Original Kings of Comedy* takes us from his inability to take care of his crack-addicted sister's children, to a nephew who makes fun of his mentally challenged bus driver, to the varied black uses of the word "motherfucker." Though Mac's performance, like Harris's BeBe skit, relies on a slanted critique of single mothering, the performance is technically still the best comedic stage performance I've seen in my lifetime.

Though few will admit it, black comedy and black comedians laid the groundwork for what would become the contemporary hip-hop emcee. Successful emcees are able to boast, confess, and critique just as efficiently as our most accomplished black comedians. The mic is their heartbeat and, like Rakim, many successful comedians are known for literally slamming the mic down when the show is over "to make sure it's broke."

Bernie Mac broke many mics and solidified himself as our very last "we" comedian. And as quiet as it's kept, we've only had three successful "we" comedians in the last thirty years: Richard Pryor, Robin Harris, and Bernie Mac. All three of these comedians seemed joyful in being there with us (which is different than being there in front of us), and though each had his own kind of cool, if at any point a heckler had interrupted his show with "Damn, Bernie (or Richard or Robin), that's some sad-ass shit you talking about," all three would have replied, "You gotdamn right," with a pointed frown on his face, "cuz I'm a sad motherfucker, you black summamabitch..." And everyone in the joint, including the heckler, would have known that Bernie was saying, "I love you, too."

In 2001, Mac was the only King of Comedy without a television show. By 2002, Mac had parlayed that great fifteen minutes into his own show on Fox. "Had I gone to another major network," he said, "I would have had to battle with them every day to get my point of view across. And I didn't feel like battling about my culture."

His culture. Our home.

Mac was reluctant to go the route of TV because he saw how it managed to water down and make caricatures of comedians like Don Rickles and Richard Pryor. Uncompromising, blue-black, bug-eyed uncles with deep Chicago twangs and a deeper love for black folks don't get networks shows, much less single-camera network shows with no laugh tracks. Bernie Mac's show was as meta as it was soulful and resilient.

Anticipating the question of how black comedians keep the edge and contour of their stand-up on network television, Bernie Mac starred as "Bernie Mac" on *The Bernie Mac Show*. And he had to. Can you imagine Mac trying to cram all of the jagged wonder he embodied on stage into some cardboard comic caricature?

Bernie Mac's TV show explored family values without prescribing family values. Like George Burns and Dobie Gillis before him, Mac's use of the confessional address to the audience within the show brought America into his house without any unexplained synthesizing of his voice. And when that voice was synthesized, "America" and Mac knew it, and we were left to critique America's consumption and/or misunderstanding of the synthetic Bernie Mac, just as we were able to critique Mac's troubled character. The show forced us to look at race, think about class, and feel gender through the lens of postmodernity, new black celebrity, new black money, new black parenting, and old-school black communal values. The show gave us a rare model of how these intersections can be navigated while producing meaningful, cutting-edge provocative art.

Around the third season of the show, we could tell something wasn't right with Bernie. His eyes didn't look right. His hair looked like it was just haphazardly placed on the top of his head. And though he still had killer comic timing, the reverberation was much less frantic and exciting. Mac still felt like our uncle, but our uncle had gotten sick. And on August 9, 2008, Uncle Bernie Mac died from complications of pneumonia.

Before he died, Bernie Mac modeled honesty. And really, that should be one of the goals of any artist. Mac stood there with us on the edge of the world suffering from physical, emotional, familial, and psychic afflictions. He showed us that we suffered together, and though we didn't have the will or the platform to say it that he had, he heard us and replied, "I love you, too."

Bernie Mac was the blackest, baddest, most loving genius uncle summamabitch to walk across this country's stage. And no matter how big he got, he always looked happy to be here with us. We loved you, Bernie Mac, for all of this and a whole lot more. You reminded us that we were never alone, and that we owed each other honest, joyful explorations of our past and present pain.

Bernie Mac once said, "A lot of my material, it comes from my pain, the loss of my parents, my family. I try to find humor in the most inopportune times. That's what keeps us alive, keeps us decent people, keeps us connected no matter what. That's comedy, man. That's comedy."

Thank you for your character, Bernard McCullough. Thank you for your pain.

III.

Prior to September 13, 1996, neither I nor anyone I knew in Jackson, Mississippi, looked up to Tupac Amaru Shakur. We heard Tupac's debut verse on Digital Underground's "Same Song" at Lerthon's house and thought he rhymed like a kid who wanted to be down. We eventually watched Tupac in *Juice* on Stacey's VCR and thought he was a watered-down O-Dog from *Menace*. We listened to Tupac's stacked vocals and were convinced he lacked the vocal gravity and lyrical imagination of Chuck D and KRS-One, or the mesmerizing psychological affliction of Scarface and Ice Cube.

While we literally thought we could rhyme at least as well as a twenty-one-year-old Tupac Shakur, when the music stopped, he refused to hit us upside the head with clumsy clichés and twinkly phraseology. He told the truth, without rhyme, unlike anyone we'd ever heard. During Tupac's first interview for MTV, Kurt Loder lobbed the trite question, "Can you tell me some of the things that someone like you who grows up in the inner city deals with?"

Tupac told him, "Our family crest was cotton. The only thing we can leave behind is culture, is music. Dignity and determination, that's what we have. I feel like I'm cheated! Instead of me fulfilling my prophecy, I have to start one. Instead of me doing a good job of carrying on an empire, I have to build one. That's a hell of a job for a twenty-one-year-old. That's a hell of a job for any youngster, male or female, to have to build an empire for your family..."

By 1994, at age twenty-three, Tupac was the reckless outlaw of his, and other's, lyrical compositions. Like too many of us, he flirted recklessly with bullets, police, money, curious women, and mean men. While the media focused on his first shooting in New York City and the eleven months he served in a correctional facility for sexually abusing a nineteen-year-old woman, something else was happening. The precision and believability of his art finally caught up with the breadth of his social vision.

Somehow, Tupac's voice, which had once seemed almost brittle to us, became an inflected instrument, one that could whisper, chant, and bellow at any point in a song. His majestic manipulation of the long "e" in words like "adversary," "crazy," "cemetery," "memories," "bury," "Hennessy," "misery," "bleed," "please," "free," "g's," "me," and of course "enemies" made millions of people believe not only in Tupac, but in his version of their truth.

Then he got shot on November 7, 1996.

I was twenty-one, four years younger than Tupac. Bullets and love had run me away from Mississippi one year earlier and I had landed in a progressive place out in the middle of some Ohio cornfields. Oberlin College was peopled with what my grandma called "good white folks." One of these good white folks, a short wobbly drunk whose name I can't remember, tapped me on my shoulder as I was coming out of the shower late one Saturday night. He told me that Tupac had been shot again in Las Vegas.

"MTV told me," he said. "It's true."

Without knowing how many times he'd been shot, where the bullets landed, how, or if, he made it to the hospital alive, even if Tupac Shakur had actually been shot, I knew he was going to die.

I didn't know much in the fall of 1996, but I knew intimately the ways that black American ambition, unchecked by healthy doses of fear, would lead to slow, painful death. This was our American story. I also knew that when enough rusty bullets were fired from traumatized citizens at moving black targets (no matter how passionate, willful, sensual, and imaginative those targets might be), the targets would eventually cease to exist.

It was inevitable.

As a grown man who now makes a living teaching and tapping on the worn screen doors of American memory and imagination, I still can't find space for a Tupac Shakur in his forties. I'd like to believe that Tupac would have gotten even better as an artist, activist, and critical citizen. But I can't figure out how someone so brilliant, so committed to honest exploration, so willing to fight for us, with us, and against us, could ever live beyond twenty-five in our United States.

Sixteen years after Tupac's death, I need help imagining how a twenty-five-year-old Tupac might have engaged with the world the day after September 11, 2001. What would that twenty-five-year-old Tupac have done after his people were left drowning in poisonous water on August 29, 2005? What would he say to the relentless American politicians on the left and right who take no responsibility for their part in our American mess? How would he touch the millions of brothers and sisters in prison-industrial complexes and the thousands of young brothers taking turns dying and killing in Chicago, Jackson, Oakland, Little Rock, New Orleans, Newark, Detroit, Gary, Poughkeepsie, and Flint?

Eerily, the 2012 Republican and Democratic national conventions ended without one mention of these American citizens or the responsibility this nation has to them. Not only would the convention speakers not talk *to* them; they refused to even talk *about* them. While many of us were beaming with joy at the speeches we heard from Michelle, Bill, and Barack, and thanking our lucky stars that Mitt Romney and his band of *Unimaginative American Thieves* were… well, obviously unimaginative American thieves, a part of me was remembering the political stars of our nation, on both the right and left, when they were twenty-five.

Bill Clinton was milling around the halls of Yale Law School hitting on a fellow student named Hillary Rodham. Barack

Obama was trying his hand at community organizing in Chicago. Michelle Robinson had just finished her first year as an associate at Sidley & Austin, a corporate law firm in Chicago. Mitt Romney was finishing up his senior year as an English major at BYU.

Strange.

By age twenty-five, Tupac Amaru Shakur had recorded six albums and starred in five movies. Five bullets had entered his body and he'd gone to prison for eleven months. He'd travelled around the world, influencing the life and art of millions of people and talking about organizing a movement against poverty and police brutality. He had shot two white off-duty cops in Atlanta who were harassing a black man, and beat the case. By age twenty-five, Tupac Shakur had fought to stay alive for six days in a Las Vegas hospital after three new bullets entered his body. And less than three months after his twenty-fifth birthday, Tupac Shakur was dead.

Strange.

I kept longing for that spooky Tupac hologram from Coachella to make an appearance at the 2012 Democratic National Convention. I didn't want the hologram to necessarily dis the president; I wanted the hologram to obliterate convenient notions of innocence, to truly democratize the audience it addressed, and to tell the truth. I literally wanted it to glide onto the stage right after President Obama riffed on citizenship. I wanted it to sit on the edge of that stage, dangling its twitching feet in front of the world with President Obama behind it.

When President Obama frowned, leaned toward the teleprompter directly in front of him, and used his disciplining-black-men voice to say, "Come on, Pac. What are you doing? Don't be a jackass." I wanted the hologram to say to President Obama what the actual Tupac Shakur had already said to us in "Smile."

"What you lookin' all sad for? Nigga, you black. Smile for me now."

And as President Obama broke awkwardly into a worried smile before getting rushed off by Secret Service, the hologram would stand up, wink his eye at our president, and walk toward the podium.

And as Secret Service rushed the president's podium and started haphazardly putting their hands, guns, and mace through the chest of the hologram, the hologram would smile and keep going. "They can't touch me," it would say. "There's no way these people can own planes and there's people who don't have houses, apartments, shacks, drawers, pants!"

The stunned audience in Charlotte, unsure whether to clap, cry, smile, or run away, would keep staring up at the hologram. Still smiling, the hologram would keep going. With a smile still on his face, but odd-shaped tears dripping out of his eyes, the hologram would float through the roof.

I know it's wrong, but I just wish the real Tupac Amaru Shakur could have never been touched. I wish we could have helped him run toward life a little while longer. Most of all, I wish we didn't ever have to look up to see Michael Jackson, Bernie Mac, or Tupac Shakur smile again.

You Are the Second Person

You know that any resemblance to real places, spaces, people, time, or things is purely coincidental.

ALONE, YOU SIT ON THE FLOOR OF YOUR APARTment thinking about evil, honesty, that malignant growth in your hip, your dead uncle, letters you should have written, the second person, and stretch marks. You're wearing an XXL T-shirt you plan on wearing the day your novel comes out. The front of the T-shirt says, "What's a real black writer?" The back reads, "Fuck you. Pay me." You open your computer. With a scary pain in your hip, you inhale and force a crooked smile before reading an email from Brandon Farley, your fifty-four-year-old black editor.

"The success of your book will be partially dependent on readers who have a different sensibility than your intended audience," he writes. "As I've already said to you, too many sections of the book feel forced for the purpose of discussing racial politics. Think social media. Think comment sections. Those white people buy books, too, bro. Readers, especially white readers, are tired of black writers playing the wrong race card. If you're gonna play it (and I think you should) play it right. Look at Tarantino. He is about to fool all these people into believing they are watching a black movie with *Django*. I guarantee you that whiteness will anchor almost every scene. That's one model you should think about.

"Also, black men don't read. And if they did, they wouldn't read this kind of fiction. So you might think of targeting bougie black women readers. Bougie black women love plot. They love romance with predictable Boris Kodjoe-type characters. Or they love strong sisters caught up in professional hijinks who have no relationships with other sisters. Think about what holds a narrative like *Scandal* together. In 2012, real black writers make the racial, class, gender, and sexual politics of their work implicit. Very implicit. The age of the 'race narrative' is over, bro. As is, the only way your book would move units is if Oprah picked it for her book club. That's not happening. Oprah only deals with real black writers."

You begin typing, "Hey Brandon, this is my fourteenth thorough revision for you in four years. I know I'm not changing your mind and that's fine. Thanks for telling me what real black writers do and what Oprah likes. You never told me you met her. Anyway, the black teenagers in my book are actually purposefully discussing 'racial politics' in awkwardly American ways. Their race and racial politics, like their sexuality and sexual politics, is somehow tied to every part of their character. My book is unapologetically an American race novel, among other things. I'm still not sure why you bought the book if you didn't dig the vision."

You push send on the email before opening up the word.doc you just defended. You jump to chapter nine. Thirty minutes later, a section of the book where an older queer coach tries to impart a strange "them/us" racial understanding to your narrator is cut because it "explicitly discusses racial politics."

You call your editor names that hurt, muddied misanthropic names you pride yourself on never calling any human being, while looking out the tall window of your second-floor apartment in Poughkeepsie, New York.

A barefoot white boy with a red and black lumberjack shirt is outside sitting under an oak tree. He's doing that walkie-talkie thing on his phone that you fucking hate. You can tell he's telling the truth and lying at the same time.

"*You fucking* hurt me more than anyone in my whole life," he says. "I couldn't hate *you*...I just don't trust *you*... *You*'re the second person who has done this to me. *You*'re the one who said you tell the truth... *You* started this." The white boy is scratching his sack with the thumb of left hand and using his big toe to make designs in the dirt in front of him. "*You* ruined my life and hurt me way more than I hurt *you*. It's always all about *you*."

You wonder about the second person on the end of the phone. Is the second person a woman or man? Is s/he listening to the lumberjack on speakerphone? Is s/he wishing the lumberjack would hurry up and finish so s/he can run and get a two-for-one special on Peanut Buster Parfaits from Dairy Queen? You know far too well why a first or third person could self-righteously claim innocence in matters of love and loss, but you can't figure out why the lumberjack is scratching his sack with his thumb and making dirt rainbows with his big toe.

Looking down at the browning "s" key on your keyboard, you think more hateful thoughts about your editor, your ex-girlfriend, skinny people, and fat young black men. These thoughts distract you from the pain in your hip, the dirt on your hands.

For five years, Brandon Farley, your editor, has had you waiting.

You remember the acidic sweetness in Grandma's voice when you told her you'd just signed a two-book deal with "KenteKloth

Books," the most popular African-American imprint in the country. New York fall felt like Mississippi winter as Grandma came out of her second diabetic coma.

"We are so proud of you, baby," Grandma whispered over the phone from Forest, Mississippi. "Just remember that God gave you five senses and whatever health you got for a reason. When they gone, they gone, but if you don't use them best you can while you got them, ain't a bigger fool in the world than that fool in the mirror."

Six months before your first novel's initial scheduled publication date of June 2009, you stopped hearing from Brandon Farley. He didn't answer your calls or respond to emails. You gave up and called the publisher of KenteKloth in February.

"Oh, Brandon didn't tell you?" his boss asked. "He's no longer with us, but your book has been picked up by Nathalie Bailey. She'll call you in a few days."

Your lungs whistled, crashed, and slipped into the heels of your feet. You told yourself it would be okay. Then you trudged your sexy ass to the International House of Pancakes.

Three hours later, you were full, fatter than you wanted to be, less sexy than you were, and you had found a way to reach Brandon Farley at home. Brandon apologized for not telling you that he wasn't seeing eye-to-eye with his boss. He promised you that Nathalie Bailey was a friend of his who would do right by both of your novels.

A week later, you got a call from Nathalie. "It's a hard sell for black literary fiction these days," she told you. "But I like what you're doing. You're on your way to becoming a real black writer. It's a gorgeous book with big messy ideas and we've got to work hard and fast. But I'd love for you to let me take this book to publication. It's a winner."

You felt a comfort with Nathalie, but you didn't want to be as impulsive as you had been with Brandon. "Can I have a few days to think about it?" you asked her. "Just to make sure."

A few days passed and you planned on calling Nathalie at 4:00 p.m. on a Thursday. At 3:00 p.m., you got a call from a 212 number. Before you had a book deal, 917 and 212 numbers were like slimming mirrors; they made you think, *Damn nigga, you ain't that disgusting at all.*

On the other end of 917 and 212 numbers were agents, editors, or an ex telling you she was sorry and she missed sharing a heartbeat.

"Hello," you answered, trying to sound busy and country at the same time.

"Hi."

It was Brandon Farley.

After a few minutes of spin where Brandon Farley showed you how much he remembered about your book and how happy he was to be the new senior editor of young adult fiction at the widely acclaimed "Duck Duck Goose Publishing Company," he said, "… all that to say, we really want your book."

"Word?"

"Word up, bro!" Brandon laughed. It was the first time any black man on earth had ever called you "bro" with a long "o."

"Bro," he said it again, "I will pay you more for one book than you got for two over at KenteKloth. I'll want an option of first refusal on the second. But that'll still give you the kind of flexibility you want."

"Are you serious?" you asked. "Only thing is I'm a little worried about changing the subtext and the darkness and the metafictive stuff if it's gonna be marketed as a young adult book. The ending ain't really pretty."

"You'd be surprised at the possibilities in young adult fiction," he told you. "Listen, bro, young adults will read it. This is adult literary fiction with mass appeal. You won't have to make many changes at all and we can get you a pub date of June 2010."

"But what about Nathalie?" you asked.

"Bro, you're the second person to ask me about her," he scoffed, sounding like a hungry hip-hop mogul. You hated even imagining using the word "scoffed."

"It's business, bro. Never personal. You'll have to get out of that contract over there. And I've got the perfect agent for you. She's this wonderful fine sister over at Chatham Ward & Associates named Bobbie Winslow. Look her up. Bobbie'll take care of everything if you decide to go with us."

You smiled and forgave him for four or five "bro's" too many.

Later that night, Bobbie, the perfect agent/fine sister, called from a 212 number and asked you to send her the other pieces you were working on. By 8:00 p.m., you'd sent her the book Brandon wanted, another novel, and a rough draft of some essays you'd been working on. By 3:00 a.m., she emailed you and said, "We want you. You're the second person I've said this to in five years, but I think you could change the trajectory of African-American contemporary literature. You've got the makings of what Brandon calls, 'a real black writer.' I'm so excited about the new projects you're working on. If you sign with Chatham Ward, we'll have our lawyers get you out of the deal with Nathalie in the next week or so and Brandon says he can get us half the advance in three weeks. I'll be in touch."

You never contacted Nathalie, but a few days later, Bobbie, the perfect agent/fine sister did. "Nathalie is so fucking pissed," she said a few days later, "but all's fair in love, war, and business." As you wondered whether this was love, war, or business, you and your perfect agent/fine sister waited and waited and waited for Brandon to deliver.

Six months later, three months after your initial publication date of June 2009, Brandon offered you substantially less money than he had promised and a publication date a year later than the one he verbally agreed to.

"Pardon me for saying this," your perfect agent said over the phone from a different 212 number, "but Brandon Farley is a bona fide bitch-ass nigga for fucking us out of thousands of dollars and pushing the pub date back to June 2011. He's just not professional. I'm wondering if this was just some ploy to get you away from KenteKloth. He's been trying to take all his authors away from them as a way of fucking the company."

"I don't get it," you said, shamefully exicted that your agent had used "fuck," "bitch-ass," and "nigga" in one conversation.

"So Brandon acquired this wonderful list of new literary black authors at KenteKloth, and they were all going to work with Nathalie after he was basically fired from the company. Nathalie and the house were going to get credit for a lot of his work. Do you get it now? We got caught up in some something really nasty."

You finally got your first edit letter from Brandon Farley the following July. In addition to telling you that the tone of the piece was far too dark and that you needed an obvious redemptive ending, Brandon wrote, "There's way too much racial politics in this piece, bro. You're writing to a multicultural society, but you're not writing multiculturally."

You wondered out loud what writing "multiculturally" actually meant and what kind of black man would write the word "bro" in an email.

"Bro, we need this book to come down from 284 pages to 150," he said. "We're going to have to push the pub date back again, too.

I'm thinking June 2012. Remember," he wrote, "It's business. I think you should start from scratch but keep the spirit. Does the narrator really need to be a black boy? Does the story really need to take place in Mississippi? The Percy Jackson demographic," he wrote. "That's a big part of the audience for your novel. Read it over the weekend. Real black writers adjust to the market, bro, at least for their first novels."

By the time you found out Percy Jackson wasn't the name of a conflicted black boy from Birmingham, but a fake-ass Harry Potter who saved the gods of Mount Olympus, you were already broken. Meanwhile, someone you claimed to love told you that you were letting your publishing failure turn you into a monster. She said that you were becoming the kind of human being you had always despised. You defended yourself against the truth and, really, against responsibility, as American monsters and American murderers tend to do, and you tried to make this person feel as absolutely worthless, confused, and malignant as you felt. Later that night, you couldn't sleep, and instead of diving back into the fiction, for the first time in your life, you wrote the sentence, "I've been slowly killing myself and others close to me, just like my uncle."

Something else was wrong, too. Your body no longer felt like your body, and you doubted whether your grandma would ever see your work before one of you died.

Two years after the original scheduled publication date for your first book, there was still no book. Questions fell like dominoes. *Why would Brandon buy the book*, you kept asking yourself. *Why would that bitch-ass nigga get you out of a contract for a book he didn't want*, your perfect agent kept asking you. *Why'd you promise stuff you couldn't deliver*, you asked Brandon on the phone.

"The book doesn't just have Duck Duck Goose's name on it," you told him, slightly aware of what happens when keeping it real goes wrong. "My name is on that shit, too. That means, on some level, it ain't business. I feel like you want me to lie. I read and write for a living, Brandon. I see the shit that's out there. I've read your other books. I see your goofy book covers looking like greasy children's menus at Applebee's. I ain't putting my name on a fucking greasy Applebee's menu. I'm not. Don't front like it's about quality. You, and maybe your editorial board, don't think you can sell this book because you don't believe black Southern audiences read literary shit. And that's fine. Maybe you're right. If you didn't believe in it, why buy it in the first place? Look, I can create an audience for this novel with these essays I've been writing," you tell him. "It sounds stupid, but I can. I just need to know that you're committed to really publishing this book. Do you believe in the vision or not?"

After a long pause during which you could hear Brandon telling his assistant, Jacques, to leave the room and get him a warm bear claw with extra glaze, he said, "Bro, you're the second person to complain to me this morning about how I do my job. The first person had a bit more tact. Honestly," he said, "reading your work has been painful. It's business. Take that folksy shit back to Mississippi. I did you a favor. Don't forget that. You're just not a good writer, bro. Good bye."

The next morning you got an email from Brandon with the following message,

"Hey Wanda, I finished the revision this afternoon. It totally kicks ass. Congrats. I've sent back a few line edits, but it's brilliant. Move over Teju and Chimamanda. There's a new African writer on the scene showing these black American writers how it's done. I'm so proud of you. Always darkest before the dawn, Wanda. It feels so empowering to work with the future of contemporary diasporic literature. Tell David hi for me. Best, Brandon."

Your name was not and never will be "Wanda."

You opened up Facebook to the News Feed page and found that Brandon, your Facebook friend, had posted the covers of recently published and forthcoming books he'd edited. Wanda's book, and all the other covers, really did look like greasy children's menus at Applebee's. Your eyes watered as you googled the published authors Brandon had signed two years after he signed you. You wanted your name on an Applebee's menu, too.

Even though you were fatter than you'd ever been and the joints in your hip got rustier and more decayed every day, parts of you were a rider. Yeah, Brandon bombed first, you thought, but right there, you felt determined to get your novel out by any means necessary so you could thank him in the acknowledgments:

"… And a special thanks to that shape-shifting cowardly ol' lying ass, Brandon Farley, the untrustworthy editing-cause-he-can't-write-a-lick-ass Tom who'd sell out his mama for a gotdamn glazed bear claw as long as the bear claw had been half eaten by a white librarian named Jacques or Percy Jackson. I know where you live. And I got goons. Can you see me now? Goooood. Congrats, BRO."

Instead you wrote, "Not sure why you sent that email intended for Wanda, Brandon. I hope we both appreciate the distinction between what's marketable and what's possible. Glad you're having success with some of your authors. I think you should give my books a chance to breathe, too. Thanks for the inspiration. Tell Wanda congratulations."

Brandon never responded to your email.

You stayed in your bedroom for weeks writing essays to your dead uncle, your grandma, the son and daughter you didn't have. Outside of that bedroom, and outside of your writing life, you'd fully become a liar *unafraid* to say I love you, *too willing* to say I'm sorry, *unwilling* to change the ingredients of your life, which meant that you'd gobbled up your own heart and you were halfway done gobbling up the heart of a woman who loved you.

One Tuesday near the end of Spring, you couldn't move your left leg or feel your toes, and you'd been sweating through your mattress for a month. You knew there was something terribly wrong long before your furry-fingered doctor, with tiny hands and eyebrows to die for, used the words "malignant growth."

"It won't be easy," the doctor told you the Friday before Spring Break. "You're the second person I've diagnosed with this today, but there's still a chance we can get it without surgery. You said you've been living with the pain for three years? Frankly, I'm worried about you," the doctor said. "You seem like you're holding something in. Fear is okay, you know? Do you have any questions?"

You watched the doctor's eyebrows sway like black wheat. They looked like a hyper four-year-old had gone buckwild with a fistful of black crayons. "I like your eyebrows," you told the doctor. "I don't know what's wrong with me. I just want my grandma to think I'm a real writer."

"I'd actually like to recommend therapy in addition to the treatment," the doctor told you before he walked you out the door.

For the next few months, you took the treatment he gave you and prided yourself on skipping the therapy. You told no one about the malignant growth in your hip, not even the person whose heart you were eating. Though you could no longer run or trust, you could eat and you could hate. So you ate, and you ate, and you hated, until sixty-eight pounds and five months later, you were finally unrecognizable to yourself.

One Sunday near the end of Spring, after talking to your two family members who were both killing themselves slowly, too, you made the decision to finally show the world the blues you'd been creating. You also decided to finish revising the novel without Brandon.

"The whole time I'd been in those woods," you wrote in one of the last scenes in the book, "I'd never stopped and looked up."

You spent the next four months of your life skipping treatments for your hip and getting a new draft of the novel done. You didn't dumb down the story for Brandon, for multiculturalism, or for school boards you'd never see. You wrote an honest book to Paul Beatty, Margaret Walker Alexander, Cassandra Wilson, Big K.R.I.T., Octavia Butler, Gangsta Boo, your little cousins, and all your teachers.

You prayed on it and sent the book to Brandon in July. You told him that you had created a post-Katrina, Afrofuturist, time-travel-ish, black Southern love story filled with adventure, metafiction, and mystery. You wanted to call the book *Long Division* after one of the characters' insistence on showing work in the past, present, and future.

"It's a book I'm proud of," you wrote in the letter attached to the manuscript. "It's something I needed to read when I was a teenager in Mississippi. Shit, it's something I need to read now. I'm willing to work on it. Just let me know if you get the vision."

Brandon responded the same day that he would check it out over the weekend and get back to you with his thoughts.

Four months later, he finally sent an email: "Ultimately, the same problems exist in this draft that were in the other drafts." Brandon ended the email, "We need more traditional adventure. We need to know less about the relationships between the characters, less racial politics, and more about the adventure. You need to explain how the science fiction works, bro. No one is going to believe black kids from Mississippi traveling through time talking about institutional racism. It's way too meandering. Kill the metafictive angle. You haven't earned the right to pull that off. This is still painful. I'm convinced you really do not want to be a real black writer, bro. The success of your book will be partially dependent on readers who have a different sensibility than your intended audience…"

Still too ashamed to really reckon with your disease or your failures, and too cowardly to own your decisions, you stretched your legs out on the floor of your living room and cried your eyes out. After crying, laughing, and wondering if love really could save all the people public policy forgot, you grabbed a pad and scribbled, "Alone, you sit on the floor…"

After writing for about two hours, you wondered why you started the piece with "Alone, you…" You are the "I" to no one in the world, not even yourself.

You've eviscerated people who loved you when they made you the second person in their lives, when they put the relationship's needs ahead of your wants. And you've been eviscerated for the same thing.

You're not a monster. You're not innocent.

You look down at the browning "s" key on your keyboard. You don't know how long you'll live. No one does. You don't know how long you'll have two legs. You know that it's time to stop letting your anger and hate toward Brandon Farley and your publishing failure be more important than the art of being human and healthy. You know it's time to admit to yourself, your writing, and folks who love you that you're at least the second person to feel like you're really good at slowly killing yourself and others in America.

"Sorry your reads have been so painful, Brandon," you start typing. "I want to get healthy. That means not only that I need to be honest, but also that I've got to take my life back and move to a place where I no longer blame you for failure. I've thought and said some terrible things about you. I've blamed you for the breaking of my body and the breaking of my heart. I really believed that you and your approval would determine whether I was a real black writer, worthy of real self-respect and real dignity.

"There was something in my work, something in me that resonated with your work and something in you. We are connected. I'm not sure what happens next. No young writer, real or not, leaves an iconic press before their first book comes, right? Whatever. I can't put my name on the book that you want written and it's apparent that you won't put your company's name on the book I want read. We tried, Brandon, but life is long and short. I've written my way out of death and destruction before. I'm trying to do it again. I think I'm done with the New York publishing thing for a while. I'm through with the editors, the agents, and all that stress. No hate at all. It's just not for me. I can't be healthy dealing with all of that. I've been cooking up a lot of stuff. I'll get my work out to my folks and if they want more, I'll show them. If not, that's fine. I'm a writer. I write.

"I'm sorry and sorrier that sorry is rarely enough. God gave me senses and a little bit of health. It's time for me to use them the best that I can. Thanks for the shot. Good luck. I hope you like the work I'm doing. Not sure if it's good, but I know it's black, blue, Mississippi, and honest. I'm a not a bro, Brandon. You ain't either. Thanks again for everything."

You look up.

You close your eyes.

You breathe.

You look down and you keep on writing, revising, and imagining, because that's what real black writers do.

Epilogue

My First Teachers—A Dialogue

DEAR KIESE,

I thank God for you. I thank him for the boy you were, the man you are, and the teacher you are becoming.

You have been a good son to your parents; you have been a great grandson and a wonderful nephew to me. What I love the most about you is that you have been a role model for young black men and black women. You have always had the courage to step over, look over, and at the same time, address with courage the wrongs in your life.

I know you have great faith in God. I love it when you call me and ask me to pray for you. It reminds me that your faith in God has not faded because of the evilness of the adversary. Always remember that what the enemy sent for bad, God will turn it for your good if you believe and keep the faith.

I have challenged you to not use profanity because you have such a reign of the English language. I know you can articulate your thoughts without cursing. In this season, you must be a voice of clarity and truth. Never be afraid to share your heart, but I want you to always guard your heart, too. Never be afraid to tell your story, but remember to tell it with grace. Never be afraid to share your pains and struggles, but share them first with God in prayer. Let him guide you as to who is entitled to the most intimate parts of you. I worry that you share with people who do not have your best interest at heart. Please be more deliberate. You will understand one day.

Set goals, write visions, dream big, and know that all things work together for the good of those who love the Lord. Never allow bitter people to make you bitter. Haters will hate. The man of courage is not the man who did not face adversity. The man of courage is the man who faced adversity and spoke to it. The man of courage tells adversity, "You're trespassing and I give you no authority to steal my joy, my faith, or my hope."

Ten seconds is too long to dwell on the negative. After nine seconds, cast your cares toward heaven and ask God to take your problems and you keep on pressing.

Psalm 91

You will not fear the terror of night, nor the arrow that
flies by day, nor the pestilence that stalks in the darkness,
nor the plague that destroys at midday.

This scripture has carried me through the most difficult seasons of my life. I hope it will bless you on your travels in life. I love you and thank God for you. It is my prayer that the blessings of God will over- take you in all of your endeavors as you allow God to order your steps. Remember, no matter what, God expects teachers to teach and learn every day of their lives. You have no choice. Reach out to your mama. She needs to hear your voice.

Love always,

Aunt Sue

DEAR MAMA,

When you pulled that gun on me at nineteen, I knew that it was because American life was eating you up from the inside, and you wanted me to live. Five years after getting kicked out of school, I was offered a teaching job at Vassar College. As Aunt Sue has said thousands of times, "The devil is a liar."

After a fourteen-hour drive from Bloomington, Indiana, I drove directly to the main gates of Vassar College and instead of going through what I knew would be the hassle of security, I thought about what you would want me to do. I turned around and found my way to Alumnae House, the college hotel.

Alumnae House was the first hotel I'd ever been in that had no televisions in the room. What Alumnae House lacked in televisions, it made up for in spooky pictures of little beady-eyed white children. All through Alumnae House, I found myself being looked at by the hollow gazes of little Brody, Chad, and Hannah.

I called Grandma from the room and told her that Vassar didn't feel like home, that I didn't like the way the little white kids were looking at me, and that I didn't like how Vassar looked like a guarded castle. Grandma said that Northern rich white folks loved to put ghost-looking pictures of white children on the walls and that I didn't drive fourteen hours to "...find no home or judge no white folks' pictures. You have a home," she told me. "You up there to get a job. Those white folks are lucky to have you applying for that job. But it's still a blessing. So get that blessing, create blessings for yourself and our people, and don't get caught up in no mess."

I got that blessing, Mama, and I also got caught up in the kind of mess that would need at least two hundred more pages to explore.

When I was twenty-five, you told me to confront failure and mediocrity with honesty, humility, and imaginative will, and to show a little more restraint with my anger since I had students of my own who would look to me as a model.

I'm still working on that.

In and out of the classroom, my kids have asked hard questions, and risked intellectual and emotional shame and fatigue. After graduating, some led renewal efforts in New Orleans; some graduated from law school; a few became producers; tons have gone on to seek MFAs and PhDs; plenty have become journalists; others are doing the colossal (and colossally underpaid) work of teaching middle school and high school. But more than anything, they're creating generative work in the world and being honest about their joys and failures. They are doing their jobs to make a crazy-making nation less crazy-making and more morally just.

I get why teachers get tired, Mama. I get why teachers punish themselves. But I also get how the students fuel us, teach us, keep us committed to life. Any supposed success I've had since I left home has been because of the prayers of my family, my memories of home, my imagination, and mostly my students. Of course, some of my students are trifling as hell, but most have accepted that they would not have the choices they have, or sturdy moral centers, were it not for the committed students who came before them. This is what you taught me. This is what I'm trying to teach my students. This is what my students teach each other.

Last week, I got an email, a tweet, and phone call from my favorite emcee, my favorite writer, and my favorite academic. It felt so good, Mama, to know that I somehow managed to live long enough to inspire folks who have spent a lifetime inspiring me. But that truth was cotton candy compared to the joy of watching Cordelia and Ocasio ask some of their one-of-a-kind questions, or Alitasha patiently breaking down the rituals of Easter at Coney Island in her thesis, or Sharon sitting in the president's conference room telling a roundtable of mostly white folks that black and brown women of color deserve more care and honesty from the institution.

I get why you teach, Mama. And I get that the love you have for your students and that your students have for you is one of the most lasting loves in the world. I didn't understand that as a child. And I hated that you were rarely home, and how we had more books than bill money, but now I get it. You had one child, but you had hundreds of students with thousands of pounds of passion. You were changing the world, and allowing yourself to be changed and loved, one student at a time.

I love you, Mama. My insides bruise easily and I'm prone to addictive tendencies when my heart hurts, just like you. I have looked fleshy, complicated love in the face and convinced myself I wasn't worthy of love or loving. I have lied. I have cheated. I have failed and I have maimed myself and others close to me. But I believe in transformation, and for the first time in my life, I really get how transformation is impossible without honest acceptance of who you are, whence you came, what you do in the dark, and how you want to love and be loved tomorrow. Baldwin wrote years ago that the only real change is a moral change.

After finishing this book, I finally get what he means.

I hope you can read this book and know that I listened and I watched. I want you to be proud of the teacher, writer, and worker that I've become. Thank you for being my first teacher. I learned, and I'm doing everything I can do to stop slowly killing myself and others in America. I'm sorry I was bad at being human for so long. I love you and I just want you, Grandma, Aunt Linda, Aunt Sue, Nicole, little Amiel, my father, my students, my state, and our people to choose life even though our nation has perfected making murder so easy.

I don't want to be a murderer any more, Mama. I choose life.

Your child,

Kiese

Acknowledgments

A VERSION OF "HIP HOP STOLE MY SOUTHERN BLACK Boy" appeared in the anthology *Longman's Hip Hop Reader*. A version of "Kanye West and HaLester Myers Are Better at Their Job" appeared in the literary journal *Mythium*. Versions of "We Will Never Ever Know," "Our Kind of Ridiculous," and "How to Slowly Kill Yourself and Others in America" appeared on gawker.com. A version of "The Worst of White Folks" appeared on ESPN.com. A version of "Eulogy for Three Black Boys Who Lived" appeared on Esquire.com. A version of "You Are the Second Person" appeared on Guernica.com. A version of "Echo" appeared on Thefeministwire.com. Versions of all of these pieces first appeared on kieselaymon.com.

I'd like to thank my aunt Sue Coleman for her contribution to my life and this book. Thank you for praying and willing yourself and our family through the sour and sweet times.

I want to thank my brothers, Darnell Moore, Kai Green, Mychal Denzel Smith, and Marlon Peterson for blessing the pages of this book with clarity, brilliance, love, and literally making our word bond.

Thank you, Linda, for wide eyes and honesty. Thanks again to my grandma, Catherine Coleman, for grace and red eyes. Thanks,

Nicole, for all that gumption. Thank you, Uncle Jimmy, for haunting me in the most beautiful ways possible. Thank you, Mama, for being proud and brilliant. You were my first teacher. I'd like to thank my father for stepping back into my life with more passion and generosity than I ever imagined. As you always say, we're in a better space.

Thank you, Professor Eve Dunbar, for superb guidance and care in the midst of professional mess, and always reminding me not to sell my work short.

Thanks to Carlos Alamo, Luis Inoa, Hiram Perez, and the entire Black and Latino Engagement Crew.

Thank you, Emma Carmichael, for that genius, space, and trust. Thanks to AJ Daulerio, Tom Scocca, Jim Cooke, and John Cook for the weekend.

Thanks to Amanda for being the best research and editorial assistant on earth.

Thanks to the art and activism of James Baldwin, Cassandra Wilson, Charlie Braxton, Josie Pickens, Margaret Walker Alexander, David Foster Wallace, Imani Perry, dream hampton, Rosa Cabrera, Sophia Chang, Heesok Chang, Matt Parker, Adisa Ajamu, Hua Hsu, Amitava Kumar, Noel Didla, and her entire Jackson crew.

Thanks to Doug, Eileen, Jali, Zach, and Agate Bolden for all that masterful work and trust.

Thanks to the inventor of the internet. You did good.

Thanks to my Facebook family and my students for being way smarter than me. I hope I didn't waste your time.

About the Author

Kiese Laymon was born and raised in Jackson, Mississippi. He graduated from Oberlin College and earned his MFA from Indiana University. Laymon is a contributing editor at Gawker.com and has written for numerous publications, including *Esquire* and ESPN.com. He is an associate professor of English and Africana Studies at Vassar College. His first novel, *Long Division*, was published by Agate Bolden in June 2013.

ALSO BY KIESE LAYMON

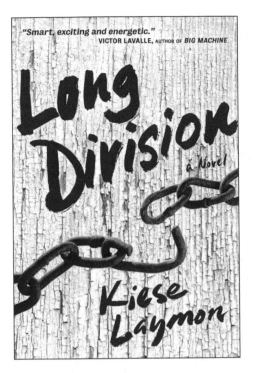

An Agate Bolden Trade Paperback Original • $15 • 978-1-93284-172-5

"Funny, astute and searching.... The author's satirical instincts are excellent. He is also intimately attuned to the confusion of young black Americans who live under the shadow of a history that they only gropingly understand and must try to fill in for themselves."

—Sam Sacks, *Wall Street Journal*

"A novel within a novel—hilarious, moving and occasionally dizzying.... Laymon cleverly interweaves his narrative threads and connects characters in surprising and seemingly impossible ways. Laymon moves us dazzlingly (and sometimes bewilderingly) from 1964 to 1985 to 2013 and incorporates themes of prejudice, confusion and love rooted in an emphatically post-Katrina world."

—*Kirkus Reviews*